ASCEND BEYOND

A Guide to Peak Performance

Kabir Mehbub

Copyright © 2024 Kabir Mehbub

Made with ❤ on the Notion Press Platform

www.notionpress.com

My Hope(Semima Parbin), It is with deep gratitude and profound love that I dedicate these pages to you. You have enriched my life in ways I never thought possible, and I am endlessly grateful for your presence by my side

Dearest

Abba & Maa,

Because of your. . .

Endurance I could bear unbearable hardship

Self-reliance I did not fall into hopelessness

Self-acceptance I appreciate my blessings and my troubles

Determination I developed a strong will to succeed

Perseverance I never gave up hope

Self- discipline I secured my future

Humility I remember my roots

Helpfulness I value friendship

Backbone I am a man

Steadfastness I could not bear to disappoint you

Vigilance I learnt not to be complacent

Invincibility I acquired inner strength

Modesty I did not get carried away by my su

ccesses. Without the Soulprints that you left me, I would not have developed the PRAISE life skills model. I would not have achieved my Break Through. I would have had a Rough Life but no Rich Life, Red Marks but no Flying Colours...

No words can express my

heartfelt love and respect for you.

Your love continues to live in all these books, and in more books yet to be written and published. In gratefulness, for all your wisdom and sacrifices.

.

Certificate

"Youngest Author to Write Maximum Number of Books Within 4 Consecutive Calander Years."

This certificate is presented to

Kabir Mehbub Alam

S/O. Mr. Ataur Rahman & Mrs. Kalpana Begum

Born On – 27/09/2003, From Assam, India.

He authored total 5 books within 4 consecutive years (2020-2023). His 1st book The Epic Poem (2020) was released on Amazon KINDLE. His 2nd book Java Fundamentals (2021) was also released on Amazon KINDLE. His 3rd book Chilled Grace (2022), 4th book Propassion: The Finance and Art of Money (2023) and 5th book The Ignited Love (2023) was released on Notion Press. All the books are of different genres.

Pranava Kumar

Founder – IWR Foundation

Priyanka Mehta	V. M. Samuel	Shadab.
Approved By	**Recorded By**	**Verified By**
Record Number: 637/24	Record ID: IWR-03/1601/24	Date: 16.01.2024

Foreword

Ascend Beyond: A Guide to Peak Performance, a convincing investigation into the immortal quest for progress and the extraordinary excursion it involves. We begin a profound investigation of what it truly means to be successful and the paths that lead us there in this book. Success, which is frequently regarded as the pinnacle of human endeavor, is a broad concept that encompasses much more than just accomplishment. It envelops development, satisfaction, and the acknowledgment of our most profound yearnings. Nevertheless, success rarely comes easily. It requests flexibility notwithstanding challenges, versatility in the midst of progress, and resolute devotion to our objectives. The process—the challenges, victories, and transformations that take place along the way—is just as important as the outcome of success in Ascend Beyond. Through the pages of this book, you will experience priceless bits of knowledge, commonsense procedures, and motivating stories that enlighten the way to individual and expert satisfaction. What separates this book is its comprehensive way to deal with progress. Here, achievement isn't bound to a particular space however is inspected from a perspective that incorporates different parts of life — vocation, connections, prosperity, and self-awareness. By embracing this extensive point of view, we uncover the interconnectedness of accomplishment across various elements of our lives. Be prepared to question your assumptions, broaden your perspectives, and discover brand-new avenues for advancement and success as you explore Ascend Beyond. This book will assist you in navigating the complexities of success, whether you are a seasoned entrepreneur, a budding professional, or simply someone looking for greater fulfillment. It provides you with invaluable wisdom as well as practical advice.

Above all else, Ascend Beyond is a demonstration of the human spirit's resilience and the limitless capacity within each of us to overcome obstacles and reach new heights. It is an invitation to go on a life-changing journey that will help you realize your potential, overcome challenges, and rise above the ordinary on your way to extraordinary success. This book is an illuminating guide that will help you chart a course toward a future marked by passion, purpose, and profound fulfillment. May it be your trusted companion on your way to success.

Embrace the journey.

Kabir Mehbub

Preface

This book is written for anyone who wants to achieve success in their life – and that must be you. Every idea and thought I share with you here is based on my own personal experiences and the knowledge I acquired reading such books and I can assure you that the practical advice I offer does work.

You have my personal guarantee that the principles I describe have brought success and happiness to me and my family and countless other people I have been fortunate enough to meet.

Now I want you to achieve the same – act upon what you read here and you too can unlock your potential for achieving success and happiness.

Kabir Mehbub

23-04-2024

Acknowledgments

Writing Ascend Beyond has been a transformative journey, and I am grateful to the many individuals whose support and contributions have made this endeavor possible.

First and foremost, I extend my heartfelt appreciation to my beloved comrade, whose unwavering belief in me has been my greatest motivation. Your encouragement and understanding have been invaluable throughout this process.

I am deeply thankful to my family and friends for their encouragement and enthusiasm. Your belief in my vision has been a source of strength.

I extend my sincere gratitude to my editor and publishing team for their guidance and expertise in bringing this book to life. Your insights have enhanced the clarity and impact of these pages.

I am grateful to the mentors and colleagues whose wisdom and support have shaped my understanding of success and personal growth.

I extend special thanks to all the individuals who graciously shared their stories and experiences, enriching this book with diverse perspectives.

Finally, to the readers—thank you for embarking on this journey with me. May the insights within these pages inspire and empower you to ascend beyond perceived limitations and achieve your own definition of success.

No thanks to
Adil Iftikar Rahman
Galif Dildar Ahmed

Misbahul Hoque
Rafique Iqbal
Asif Ahmed
Sohail Sabbir
Ruhul Amin Laskar
Ruhul Imtiaz Talukdar

Introduction

One of the hardest concepts to define is success: it means quite different things to different people. Whatever it might mean to you, this book shows you how to achieve your ultimate desire to become a success in your own terms.

Sadly, the vision of success has been adulterated by the media through their continual thirst for sensation and glamour. The majority of us have been conditioned to believe that success is totally related to money. To have millions and the trappings of so-called success, such as Rolls-Royces, jets and lots of money such that resonates in paradise, is a common perception of what success is all about.

Moreover, success is held to be limited to those who reach the pinnacle in their chosen sport, or individuals who gain power in politics, industry or commerce. Parents who raise their children in a secure and happy home, or the managers who develop their staff to greater achievement and reward, often appear to be ignored.

Success for one person might be just to get the next meal, success for another might be to gain employment in a secure job, for another freedom from worry. Success for the vast majority of us, though, is to achieve our goals, to live in a state of happiness and to have respect from those around us. So you must be the judge and jury of what success means to you. I make no apology for the fact that many of the ideas and concepts in this book are not new. They are the great principle of success. In my thirst for a greater understanding of human achievement, I have learnt much through reading and listening to others wiser and more successful than me.

I have personally used the ideas and concepts from, and have been fortunate to teach, the ascend beyond system and share it with countless other people who have also achieved great wealth and success. The many stories and analogies throughout the book are used to drive home ideas, systems and messages that lead to success.

1. The Route to Success

I promise you that this book will help you achieve the success that you desire, as long as you remember that being an unhappy success is meaningless. Whatever you do, do not make excuses – you know the old expression 'a bad workman always blames his tools'? I have heard people say, 'I'm too old', others, 'I'm too young', 'I didn't go to the right school', 'I didn't go to university' or even 'I was born under the wrong birth sign'. These are just a few of the thousands of excuses that are used to justify non-achievement.

If you want to use the principles to create financial security or make the proverbial 'million', follow the stages. The vast majority of the principles are not new, but I know that they work because they have worked for me and for many others. Do not dismiss them, undervalue them or treat them with cynicism. We all live in a world steeped in massive negativity, which can be seen in news programmes, the media and, of course, in other individuals. We are conditioned to become more cynical and sceptical about the enormous opportunities and possibilities in this incredible world in which we live and work.

WHAT IS HAPPINESS?

So let us examine what causes people to be happy. Fundamentally, happiness is achieved in three ways: first, by having something to look forward to; secondly, by sharing; and thirdly, by making somebody else happy

Looking forward to something

First, have something to look forward to. Have you ever experienced buying a new car? It might be brand new or second-hand. Your car is due to arrive in three days' time and you are excited. Two days to go, excitement increases, the arrival is getting closer. The day before, and perhaps even the night before, the excitement has increased even further. You may have difficulty going to sleep. The new car arrives. That first day, of course, pleasure, enjoyment and happiness – lots of playing with the gadgetry and equipment, and every care is taken to make sure the car does not get dirty. Each time you park and walk away, you look back to make sure it hasn't moved! Two weeks later, how do you feel about the car? Yes, your attitude has changed – the car is now just another car. Pleasure rarely comes from the owning or the having – it comes from looking forward to owning it. This applies to almost anything, from holidays to watching a television programmeto meeting a loved one to getting promoted.

We continually see on our Mobile and in NEWS the horrors of human conflict and deprivation. But surely the worst sight of all is a human face without hope. For you, my readers, there is no excuse for you not to have hope.

Sharing

Let's take the second base for happiness: sharing. Imagine going out for a delightful meal at an Indian restaurant. To start, picture a plate of mouthwatering crispy samosas filled with spiced potatoes and peas, served with tangy tamarind chutney. As your main course, envision a fragrant and flavorful butter chicken, with tender pieces of chicken simmered in a creamy tomato-based sauce, accompanied by fluffy basmati rice and warm garlic naan bread. For dessert, indulge in a traditional Indian sweet like gulab jamun—soft, syrup-soaked dumplings that melt in your mouth. What a meal! However, sit and eat that meal on your own and it's not much fun; certainly it creates very little happiness, and somehow the food does not taste the same as it would if you were sharing that meal with another person on the other side of the table to chat to.

So, sharing really does provide happiness. Now, many of us are fortunate enough to share our lives with a partner, while others find at some stage in their lives that, maybe through separation or bereavement, they are once again on their own. Does this mean the future is one of unhappiness? No, of course not. Most people have wonderful friendships and a wonderful family with whom they can share some of their time, joys and happiness. Many people gain tremendous happiness through sharing their life with a pet. The pet becomes a purpose for living, a reason for getting out of bed, and, of course, a great source of company for people on their own.

May I remind you of a saying that will be repeated later in this book... "*A joy that is shared is a joy that is doubled, a worry that is shared is a worry that is halved.*"

Making someone else happy

Third is making someone else happy. It is almost impossible not to be happy when you are making someone else happy. It is impossible not to be successful while helping to make someone else successful, and many successful businesspeople have proved, intentionally or otherwise, that by helping other people to be more financially successful, they have in turn enhanced their own wealth.

As a child, you look forward to birthdays and other festivals, obviously because these are times for surprises and presents. As you become more mature, the excitement and pleasure really come from the giving of these surprises and presents. Walk down a street sometime and smile – it is funny how people smile back. Notice how that makes you feel. As a parent, or even as a fellow human, it is wonderful to be able to give somebody else some good news – you can get so much pleasure out of that simple exercise.

Looking in the right direction

In recent years, there has been a notable surge in the popularity of gambling apps and fantasy sports platforms like Teen Patti and Dream11, particularly in conjunction with major events like the Indian Premier League (IPL). These platforms have captured the attention of countless individuals, who see them as potential avenues to quickly accumulate wealth and achieve financial success. The allure of these quick-money schemes, often fueled by the excitement of major sporting events like the IPL, can be irresistible to those seeking rapid financial gains.

The IPL, widely regarded as one of India's most renowned sporting events, has garnered attention not only for its widespread appeal but also for the less-than-scrupulous practices that accompany it. The immense sums of money involved in the IPL, driven largely by betting and speculative investments, have contributed to its fame and notoriety. Many individuals are drawn to these betting platforms, hoping for a chance to strike it rich overnight.

The desire for rapid wealth, coupled with the perception of success tied to financial gains, often leads people down a precarious path. The belief that quick riches equate to success can cloud judgment and fuel reckless behavior. In the pursuit of monetary gain, individuals may overlook the inherent risks and consequences associated with gambling and speculative investments. Unfortunately, the quest for fast and effortless wealth can quickly devolve into a cycle of disappointment and loss. What begins as a hopeful endeavor to improve one's financial standing can morph into a dangerous obsession driven by greed. The seductive promise of immediate success blinds individuals to the realities of responsible financial management and the importance of sustainable wealth-building practices. It is essential to recognize that true success is not measured solely by monetary wealth or material possessions. Success encompasses personal fulfillment, well-being, and the achievement of meaningful goals. Adopting a mindset that equates success with quick financial gains can lead to disappointment and disillusionment.

Ultimately, the pursuit of success should be grounded in principles of integrity, perseverance, and responsible decision-making. Rather than chasing elusive shortcuts to wealth, individuals can cultivate lasting success by investing in their skills, nurturing meaningful

relationships, and making prudent financial choices that align with their long-term aspirations.

When money is amassed through personal endeavour in whatever form, pleasure and happiness are achievable. In most cases when money is earnt through endeavour, it does not come in a single rush – the get-rich-quick scenario. Money comes gradually, which provides the individual with an opportunity to learn how to manage money.

PUT MONEY ON YOUR OWN SUCCESS

In this book, your hope will not be based upon a get-richquick success. Your hope will be based upon realities you can achieve.

The odds of your achieving your own success are better than you will ever be offered by any form of gambling because the odds for you are evens. The chance of a jackpot win on the lottery is approximately 16 million to 1, a win on an IPL Match might be 2 to 1, but the chance of your winning in your own life are evens. You can be successful or not – the choice really is yours.

Help others and help yourself

One of the amazing, yet fascinating, realities of successful people is that they rarely achieve success on their own. Success is usually achieved with the support, encouragement, enthusiasm, advice and help of others. It is equally true that the key to achieving what you want is to help enough people to get what they want first. It is then an absolute guaranteed certainty that you cannot fail to be successful.

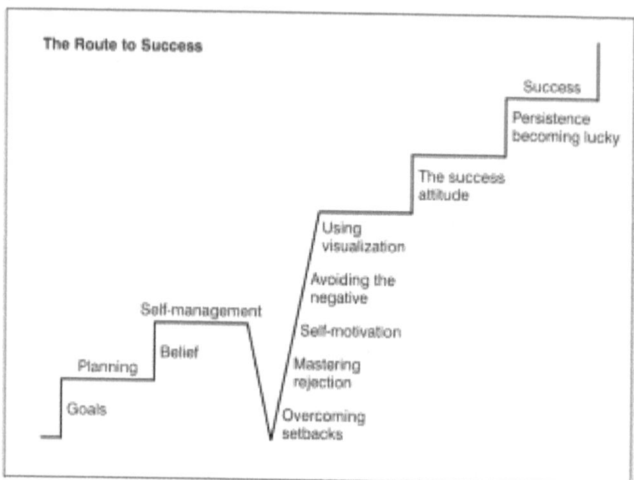

In order to achieve true success (maybe through financial independence, security, success in your profession or some outstanding sporting achievement), you must ensure that your ultimate goals will make you happy, or they will have little purpose. Throughout this book, when success is mentioned, it is intrinsically linked to happiness – success without happiness is not success.

You can be, and I believe you will be, a winner: successful, wealthy, loved and respected, by practising the philosophy and principles in *Ascend Beyond*. Yes you can!

2. Vision

Let me ask you, what do you consider to be your most valuable asset? Could it be your home, your car, your savings. The truth is, of course, that none of these is truly valuable.

Your most valuable asset is you: your mind. Everyone wants their assets and valuables to be secure. This chapter looks at how you can value and protect your most valuable asset.

I was raised to believe that security was attained through becoming a doctor, particularly by excelling in the National Eligibility cum Entrance Test (NEET). For much of the recent past, this notion held true, especially in India where becoming a doctor was seen as a prestigious and secure career path. However, in contemporary times, this perspective has evolved due to the changing landscape of medical education and employment.

Securing a spot in a reputable medical college through cracking NEET has become increasingly challenging and competitive in India. NEET, the standardized entrance exam for medical courses, demands rigorous preparation and exceptional performance. The vast syllabus, coupled with intense competition among aspiring candidates, creates a daunting environment for those aiming to pursue a career in medicine.

In the past, becoming a doctor was often viewed as a guaranteed pathway to financial security and stability. However, the current reality is different. The availability of job opportunities, post-graduation prospects, and the evolving healthcare industry dynamics have shifted the narrative. Many aspiring doctors recognize that the conventional notion of lifelong job security in medicine is no longer assured.

Given these changing circumstances, individuals are encouraged to prioritize the protection and development of their own skills and abilities. Rather than relying solely on the traditional path of securing a medical degree, it is essential to focus on nurturing one's talents and leveraging them effectively. By harnessing our inherent capabilities and potential to their fullest extent, we can enhance our personal security, well-being, and overall quality of life.

Embracing this perspective invites a shift towards a more proactive and empowered approach to career development and personal growth. Instead of placing undue emphasis on external factors like job stability, individuals are encouraged to cultivate resilience, adaptability, and a diversified skill set. This strategic mindset not only enhances individual security but also fosters a sense of fulfillment and autonomy in navigating the complexities of today's professional landscape.

Imagine acquiring a new car. Before you start driving it for the first time, it's important to understand what kind of car you have and what it's capable of. You familiarize yourself with the controls, locate where the turn signals and horn are, and test the brakes to ensure they work well. You adjust the seat position for comfort and check important things like oil levels, tire pressure, and how much fuel is in the tank.

Now, let's say this car is a small Mercedes Smart Car. Could you take this car on a long journey from one city to another, like from Mumbai to Delhi? Yes, you could, but you would need to prepare differently compared to a shorter trip, like from Mumbai to Pune.

Similarly, when you're starting a new phase or journey in your life—whether it's a new job, moving to a different city, or pursuing a big goal—it's essential to take stock of what resources and skills you have. Just like preparing for a car journey, you assess your readiness and capabilities before embarking on your next life journey. This involves understanding your strengths, skills, and the resources available to you, so you can plan and prepare effectively for the challenges and opportunities ahead.

AUDIT YOUR OWN PERSONAL ASSETS AND LIABILITIES

Every limited company, once a year, commissions its auditors to prepare statutory accounts, and within these accounts, assets and liabilities are clearly listed. I want you to carry out your own personal audit.

Before that let's understand the different types of assets : Tangible and intangible assets are two different types of assets that businesses and individuals own and use to generate value. Here's an explanation of each:

1. Tangible Assets:

Tangible assets are physical assets that have a definite physical form and can be seen and touched. These assets are typically used in the operations of a business to generate revenue. Examples of tangible assets include:

- Property, Plant, and Equipment (PP&E): This includes land, buildings, machinery, vehicles, and equipment used in production or operations.

- Inventory: Raw materials, work-in-progress goods, and finished products that a business holds for production or sale.

- Cash and Cash Equivalents: Physical currency, coins, and balances in bank accounts.

Tangible assets are recorded on a company's balance sheet at their historical cost less accumulated depreciation (for assets with a limited useful life) or impairment losses. They provide a certain level of security and can be relatively easy to value and sell.

2. Intangible Assets:

Intangible assets, on the other hand, lack a physical form and are not typically seen or touched. These assets represent valuable rights or benefits that contribute to a company's long-term value and competitive advantage. Examples of intangible assets include:

- Intellectual Property: Patents, trademarks, copyrights, and trade secrets that protect inventions, brand names, creative works, and proprietary information.

- Goodwill: The premium paid for an acquired company over its fair market value, representing the value of its reputation, customer relationships, and other intangible factors.

- Software: The cost of purchasing or developing software applications used to support business operations.

- Customer Relationships: The value associated with customer loyalty, brand recognition, and customer satisfaction.

Intangible assets are typically harder to value than tangible assets and are recorded on the balance sheet at their acquisition cost or fair market value. Unlike tangible assets, intangible assets often provide future economic benefits over an extended period, and their value may be subject to impairment testing regularly.

In summary, tangible assets are physical assets that can be seen and touched, such as buildings, equipment, and inventory, while intangible assets lack physical substance but provide value through rights and benefits like intellectual property, goodwill, and customer relationships. Both types of assets are essential for businesses and individuals to generate income and build value over time.

MY TANGIBLE ASSETS	
ASSETS	LIABILITIES

MY INTANGIBLE ASSETS	
ASSETS	LIABILITIES

First of all, create the tangible asset and liability statement. List on one side your current assets. These will include your home, car, possessions, investments, shares, etc. On the other side, list your liabilities: an overdraft or loan, unpaid bills or perhaps a hire purchase agreement.

Now repeat the exercise, setting out your intangible asset and liability statement. On one side, list your personal strengths and qualities, skills and achievements, your qualifications, your experiences, physical health and fitness, how you think your friends, family and social contacts may feel about you and so on. On the other side, list your liabilities. These could be personal weaknesses such as fear of rejection, complacency, a tendency to procrastinate or a lack of self-discipline.

You will see the importance of these two exercises in the upcoming chapters Like most people, you may well undervalue your most valuable asset: your mind. It is almost impossible to put a monetary figure on its worth – the courts have tried for years in insurance and damage claims most of us totally undervalue the most incredible piece of equipment that we were born with. Your wealth, security, happiness and success will be very much dependent upon how you use what you already have.

Preparing for a new challenge

Many people fail to prepare themselves for new challenges and opportunities for achieving wealth and happiness. Those who do achieve are continuously learning, changing and developing, being trained and coached, seeking out new ideas. The fact that you are reading this book shows that you are one of these people who have the desire to progress. *The grass is not always greener on the other side; the answer does not always lie somewhere else.*

REMOVING YOUR LIABILITIES, ENHANCING YOUR ASSETS

Look back at your list of intangible liabilities. The items need not remain there permanently – that depends entirely on you because you have the most incredible equipment planted directly between your ears, which can do anything if it really wants to. Your brain is more powerful than any computer that humankind will ever create. The greatest developments in the future are not going to be in the form of new technology, data processing, modes of travel or communication. They are going to come from increased use of the human brain.

HOW TO LOOK AFTER YOUR ASSETS

If the brain is so important, how should you look after it? Throughout this book I will be referring to the information you put into your brain and the expectations that you have of it. Although the brain is not a muscle, it does work like a muscle in some ways, the more it is used, the fitter it becomes and the better it performs. First, the brain works better with healthier blood circulation. It requires oxygen from the blood system to be pumped through it. The amount of oxygen is increased through exercise. I have found that when I am taking exercise and my body is fitter, my brain becomes less stressed, it makes better decisions, is more able to cope and is more relaxed. It responds instead of simply reacting, and I generally feel better.

The more the brain is used, the stronger it becomes. School, Colleges and Universities create the right conditions for minds to meet; where people can discuss and challenge each other's thoughts and research. In such an environment, the brain is nurtured.

Having the right qualifications

Many organizations, quite understandably, look for qualifications and academic achievement because these prove that the individual not only has a willingness to learn, but also has a powerful retention factor. This can provide an indication of someone's intelligence, but does not indicate common sense, attitude or an ability to communicate. Put all these together and you really do have a power to be reckoned with, a person highly sought-after by employers.

Logic and creativity

We all process information differently (as we will see in the chapter on communication), but our thought processes can be defined as falling roughly into two groups: left brain, giving rise to a convergent thinker for whom logic is paramount; and right brain, resulting in a divergent thinker for whom creativity is the more powerful influence.

To determine what type of thinking you use, please look at the five shapes overleaf and circle the one you instinctively find most attractive.

Shape 1

Shape 2

Shape 3

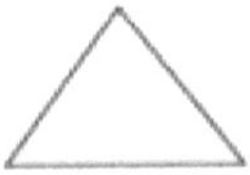

Shape 4

Shape 5

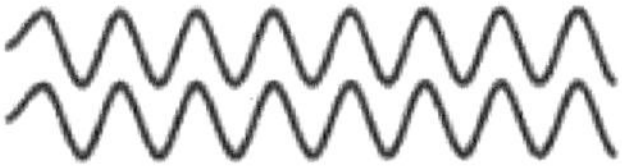

Shape 1: An extremely left-brain and logical thinker. This type of thinker is normally very methodical and utilizes logic for its own sake. As a rule, he or she is quite able and prepared to work alone.

Shape 2: This type of thinker is also very logical, although a little more flexible in his or her thinking, and prefers to work as part of a team.

Shape 3: Predominantly a logical thinker, but observe the shape. This person will use logic to make a decision, provided it takes them or their operation upwards and onwards. This person is always aiming to go forward.

Shape 4: A predominantly right-brain and creative thinker. Looking at the shape, you can see that this person keeps rolling along and bouncing back.

Shape 5: Predominantly an extremely right-brain and creative thinker. This person can be the master of the unexpected and a snappy or unconventional dresser.

The purpose of this exercise is really a little bit of fun and probably only tells you what you already know, but nevertheless, it will help you in establishing what sort of thinker you really are.

INVESTING IN YOURSELF

The body's prime function is to transport the brain. The majority of us spend vast amounts of money on the care and appearance of this transportation system, but it is quite extraordinary how mean we can be to the brain.

One of the best investments you can ever make is in yourself. Take yourself to a lecture or a seminar. Expose your brain to new thoughts, radical thinking and knowledge. Give your brain the opportunity to read. Let your brain learn from videos and Podcasts. The small cost is an investment from which you and your family can reap untold rewards.

It is great to see so many people buying more and more books on fiction, sports, fitness and other hobbies. The investment that you make in a self-help or personal development book can bring untold rewards of success in the future. Feed your brain with knowledge – it has a great thirst for usable information. Most people spend a great deal of time travelling in cars, buses, trains or aeroplanes – time which is usually wasted. So, turn your car into a learning centre and put an audiobook into your personal stereo. Listen to business and educational learning Videos or Podcasts. Change this wasted time to productive and achievement time. The extraordinary thing about playing personal development Audiobooks is that you are continuously hearing something new. Many of those I carry with me I have listened to 30 or 40 times over the years, and I cannot recall an occasion when I have not heard something new. The words themselves have never changed, but as my experiences, mood and thoughts change, so does the information I draw from them.

I finish this chapter by repeating that you have the equipment for success and happiness. The greater part of this book is devoted to showing you how to use this asset (equipment) so that it will deliver to you your hopes and dreams. It is your responsibility, and I mean your responsibility, to value and take care of this incredible tool.

Pocket Reminders

- Consider your most valuable asset – yourself
- Audit your *tangible* assets and liabilities
- Audit your *intangible* assets and liabilities
- Prepare for a new challenge
- Look after your assets
- Keep your brain in good shape: take regular exercise
- Invest in yourself: listen to CDs and read books that develop the mind.

If we did all the things we were capable of, we would literally astound ourselves.- Thomas A. Edison

3. Believe in Yourself

Let me ask you a question: how do you see yourself? Or, to put it another way, what is your self-image?

No doubt you can respond quite quickly, but now spend a little bit of time really thinking about yourself. Not about what others may think of you, because they may have completely the wrong impression, but how you actually see yourself.

Some people, as they achieve success in life, build their ego and then have an insatiable appetite to feed this ego. It is important for us all to have an ego, but not an ego problem. There is a saying: the bigger the ego, the smaller the bank balance. I remember my mother always telling me during my childhood days, *'Be nice to people on the way up, because you meet the same ones on the way back down again.'* It is very useful advice. Looking at my own experiences to date, I have had some amazing highs and some equally incredible lows, and that little message has stood me in good stead.

SELF-IMAGE

Your self-image is the key to your success. You will perform exactly as you see yourself, so your opinion of yourself is extremely important if you are aiming for success. We have all heard the expression 'Some people are their own worst enemy.' It is true; they really are. Sometimes people experience an inferiority complex and, if we're honest, we have all experienced that at some stage in our lives or in certain situations. Poor self-image is a more fundamental problem than the occasional feeling of inferiority. A person with a poor self-image communicates their negativity in their dealings with others. No doubt you have seen, or perhaps currently have, friends who are under pressure: marital problems, stress at work, redundancy, depression and, of course, poor self-image. These things are apparent in how they look and in what they say. Their appearance is not cared for: less attention is paid to hair, make-up, cleanliness and body odour. Some people overeat and become obese. It can affect their posture and the way they walk. They may even avoid people and become withdrawn. Some of the problems I have described above are things that can honestly and justifiably be explained as 'outside the individual's control'. There are events that happen and are sometimes outside our immediate control, but there are also self-inflicted, avoidable pressures

Perpetuating a poor self-image

It is important to understand that poor self-image is usually self-perpetuating. Our behaviour tends to be repetitive, the continual replaying of old patterns. The cure is simple: you must change the way you see yourself. Most people are unaware of or choose not to accept the need to change. Some, quite extraordinarily, appear to gain some weird kind of satisfaction by wallowing in their own self-pity and this, to a certain extent, becomes security for them. Success and achievement frighten them because they spend so much of their time thinking about their situation that to break out of the pattern becomes too hard to do and their confidence and self-image plummet even further.

WHAT GOES INTO YOUR BRAIN?

In Chapter 2, we talked about our brain being our greatest asset. For the purpose of this example, I would now like to describe it in its purest and simplest form as being like a box.

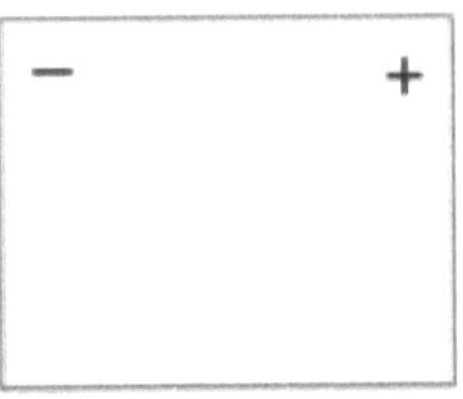

– Negative input What people say about me. What I think about myself.	+ Positive input What people say about me. What I say about myself.

Into that box are placed experiences and information that are both negative and positive. Obviously some experiences and information will not fall into either category. It could be information that we have gained, but which we may not yet have any particular use for. I would put such information on the positive side

HOW WE ARE CONDITIONED

We have all been conditioned by our life experiences, so our reactions, thoughts, feelings, emotions, image, confidence and so on are mainly developed through three forms of conditioning: our childhood, our environment and how we deal with past experiences. However, the fact that we have been conditioned is not a reason to accept where we are, nor is it an excuse for us not to try to change; and it is most certainly not a basis upon which you can say, 'Well, that rules me out from achieving what I want.' If you understand and use your past conditioning positively, dealing with it can be one of those stages on your success map.

Childhood

First of all, we are conditioned by our childhood. Every child is born with a positive brain. In the early weeks and months of any baby's life, parents are very supportive, motivational and encouraging. They are always smiling at their newborns, as are visitors and family friends. In the past, it was believed that babies were born with impaired eyesight; this, we now know, is not strictly true. There is evidence that babies can even see when inside their mother's womb. After a few weeks of life seeing parents' and visitors' faces all smiling at them, they respond with a smile. The first one or two may be of a windy sort, but then the real smiles come through. Parents now continually inject confidence and belief into their children by means of statements like 'You can crawl', 'You can speak', 'You can walk'. This is all positive conditioning. The day their child is fully mobile is often the day the positive conditioning ceases. It is no longer 'You can do it.' It is 'You can't', 'You shouldn't', 'Don't touch', 'Come here!'

Many children, throughout their childhood years, experience poor-quality teachers who do not motivate or encourage them. Some parents or teachers even say to children, 'You're useless', 'You're stupid', 'You'll never be a success', continously dwelling the negativity. Our childhood experiences naturally condition our brain and affect the way we respond and react to future situations.

Environment – who we mix with

The second form of conditioning is a form of environmental conditioning. Whatever environment you are in, over a period of time you are likely to conform to it. It is said that if you only mix with millionaires, it is virtually impossible not to become one. We have all heard parents say, 'Don't let that child get into bad company.' Why? Because a child from a safe and secure, well-behaved family who chooses to mix with hoodlums will almost certainly become one. As we believe that a person's life is formed during their first seven years.

As adults, we are consciously and subconsciously conditioned by our environment. Have you noticed that football managers seem to wear the same sort of clothes and all chew gum and move their heads in a particular way when they are being interviewed? Can you tell the difference between people who work in the public sector and those who work in the private sector? You will have experienced totally different behaviour from family, friends, colleagues and yourself as you move in different environments.

Environmental conditioning permeates every part of society and affects every one of us both positively and negatively. We naturally try to conform to the environment in which we are operating. At one extreme, people will change their appearance and even spend vast sums of money to fit into a particular environment. We are all born to be positive and conditioned to be negative. The world in which we live creates a negative effect which hampers positive success

For those of my readers who are parents, be aware that there has been continual erosion of correct pronunciation and use of the English language within schools and the communities that our young people mix in. It is, and always will be, a prerequisite for people hoping to advance in their careers, maximize their potential or be given the responsibility of leadership to be able to speak well with the right pronunciation and with a greater command of their language. Help your young people achieve this ability.

HOW TO BUILD YOUR SELF-IMAGE

Let us now move forward and look at how we can build and maintain a healthy self-image, which in turn builds selfconfidence.

1. No more excuses

Never make an excuse to try to justify your failure to achieve your goals, ambitions and success. They are what they are: excuses, not justifications.

2. Have pride in yourself

Take another look at those intangible assets that you wrote down earlier in this chapter. This is who you are and what you have to offer. Just look at the physical and mental attributes you have. Have faith and belief in yourself, and give your brain a chance to perform. You are good and you are going to get better.

3. Take care of your appearance

Have you really looked in the mirror lately – and I don't mean a superficial check-over? Do you really look successful? Is your appearance giving the image of the person you would like to be? If the outside looks good, it will really help you to feel good inside. How often have we heard people say, 'I feel so much better' after having their hair restyled or buying some new clothes – they even seem to have a greater air of self-confidence.

4. Check what you allow into your brain

Imagine a filter or a sieve that prevents certain unpleasant thoughts getting through. Do not allow other people to sabotage your assets or your success and, equally, do not do it yourself. If you catch yourself in self-destruct mode, say to yourself, 'I'm not going to think that', and replace that negative thought with a positive one, just as you would go through a punnet of strawberries picking out bad ones – discard the rotten thoughts. It takes a little bit of practice and, in some cases, courage and determination, not to think negatively.

5. Believe you can

Belief is a powerful word. It is used predominantly within a religious context. As I respect all true believers, I do not consider that I have the right to say that one religion is right and another is wrong. People throughout history have followed others with belief and conviction.

Linford Christie became the 100-metre Olympic champion at 34 years of age. Did he have a better body than the other athletes? Or was he younger than the other athletes? No.

He achieved Olympic and world success by overcoming the opinions of highly intelligent 'experts' who said he was too old; they believed that, past the age of 24, the body was incapable of running at that speed. But Linford Christie believed he could. And the same goes for football legends Cristiano Ronaldo and Lionel Messi.

6. Make positive statements

Speak positively. What we normally do is the reverse. For example, if you say, 'I'm not feeling very confident', what happens? You get exactly that result. Another example is 'I'm not feeling very well' – say that, and you will feel that way as a result. So reverse the messages from the negative to the positive and you will be giving positive instructions to your brain. Every personal development teacher, trainer or coach always stresses the importance of making positive affirmations. These powerful statements create tremendous impact on the subconscious, and it is even more effective when these positive statements are said just before going to sleep and then are repeated first thing in the morning.

7. Do not fear mistakes

It is impossible to make a mistake if you do absolutely nothing, but of course if you do absolutely nothing, you achieve absolutely nothing as well. Mistakes, errors or what some people might even term failures are, of course, only 'unsatisfactory results'. Every mistake is an experience from which you can gain information and, if you are sensible, can help build a successful future.

It is very easy for executives to get into the 'no-decision syndrome': the trap of being so fearful of making an error that they actually fail to make any decisions. All the greatest success stories have involved some mistakes. Some entrepreneurs actually claim that they have made more mistakes and errors than good decisions, but that the successful decisions have greatly outweighed the errors.

8. Do some charitable work

Let's go back to one of the original principles: that it is impossible not to be successful if you are helping other people to get what they want. If only every unemployed person would spend a little of their time in charitable work, particularly helping others less fortunate, they would automatically do themselves a dramatic favour in building their self-esteem, confidence, image and belief, and that alone would help them towards their own employment prospects.

Try to devote a little time towards helping others, even though you may be extremely busy or already highly successful. That little bit of time spent will help build your own self-belief, image and confidence.

9. Check your environment

If you are continually mixing with people who destroy your confidence, are very negative or maybe cynical and disparaging about success and achievement, move out of that environment and try to mix with people who are positive, enthusiastic and who are 'builders' rather than 'takers'. Mixing with people who are success-orientated will again make it virtually impossible for you not to be successful.

10. Compile a 'success record'

Go back to your earliest memory of success – perhaps when you were at school – and from that earliest memory, compile a record of every successful experience you have had, in both your business and your personal life. This information can be stored in a scrapbook with photographs, letters and cuttings. Apart from anything else, it is very enjoyable to do and interesting for your family, but most importantly of all, in times of self-doubt or even loss of confidence, this record will help to re-establish your shaken self-belief.

If you only look at what it is, you might never attain what it could be

 —Bits and Pieces

4. Luck

The truth is that luck is available for you; maybe not in the way that you wish, but you can become lucky. Let us start to put this into some sort of perspective. No doubt you have seen or listened to an interview with a successful actress or actor, singer or model. They nearly always say, 'Well, I was lucky' or 'I just had a little bit of luck'. Surely what they are really saying is 'I made an effort, got off my backside and got myself into the right place at the right time.'

It seems that every successful person always claims that he or she had a bit of luck. May I suggest that this is modesty. It is also interesting that people who classify themselves as unsuccessful attribute their lack of success to bad luck. We must therefore understand and distinguish between luck and chance, as there really is a very big difference.

THE 'LUCK PRINCIPLE'

The simplest and most direct explanation of luck I have come across is as follows:

L	Labour
U	Under
C	Correct
K	Knowledge

Labour

The first word may not appear to be highly motivational because it implies work, but what it really means is 'do something'.

Correct knowledge

So, what is correct knowledge? Correct knowledge is:

○ Knowing where you are today.
○ Knowing where you want to be or go. and
○ Having a plan.

The first stage in establishing correct knowledge is to make a completely honest assessment of where you are today. You will already have audited your own personal assets and liabilities in Chapter 2. You will have listed your strengths, weaknesses, assets, experiences, knowledge and contacts, and generally considered what you have to offer. So, to know where you are today is to have a sense of pride in yourself that corresponds with reality

The second stage is knowing where you want to go. We have all heard the cliché *A person going nowhere normally gets there.'* In upcoming chapters I will look specifically at how to set your goals and how to decide what those goals should be; how to have purpose, how to always have something to look forward to.

You must have goals. There is not one successful person in the history of humankind who has not achieved their success by consciously or subconsciously having purpose and goals. So, for you to be lucky, goals are essential. If you omit goals from your action plan you will be dependent on chance.

The third and final stage of correct knowledge is having a plan to achieve these goals.

Again, let me remind you that every achievement has come through visualizing goals and by carrying out a systematic plan to achieve these goals. So, if you really do want to use the 'luck principle', remember you do not become lucky by sitting on your backside.

uck and success are intricately linked in the narrative of achievement. While luck can certainly play a role in opening doors or presenting opportunities, it is often hard work, dedication, and perseverance that ultimately lead to sustained success. The interplay between luck and effort is a dynamic and nuanced aspect of the journey towards achieving one's goals.

It is undeniable that luck can sometimes be a deciding factor in an individual's success story. Serendipitous encounters, fortunate timing, or unexpected breaks can certainly contribute to propelling someone towards their desired outcomes. Famous entertainers, like the Spice Girls, may attribute some of their success to luck when reflecting on pivotal moments in their careers. However, a deeper examination often reveals the immense amount of hard work, preparation, and commitment that preceded these fortunate opportunities.

Similarly, in the world of sports, legendary golfer Arnold Palmer famously remarked, "The harder I work, the luckier I get." This sentiment underscores the notion that luck often favors those who are prepared and willing to put in the necessary effort to capitalize on opportunities. Palmer's remark encapsulates the idea that success is not merely a matter of chance but is instead rooted in diligent practice, continuous learning, and a relentless pursuit of excellence.

While luck may open doors or provide fortunate breaks, it is ultimately hard work and perseverance that sustain long-term success. Success is not solely determined by external circumstances or chance occurrences; rather, it is the result of deliberate action, strategic decision-making, and a steadfast commitment to one's goals. Individuals who attribute their success solely to luck may overlook the countless hours of effort and sacrifice that paved the way for their achievements.

Moreover, relying solely on luck can be a risky proposition. Luck is unpredictable and fleeting, whereas hard work and dedication are within one's control. By investing in their skills, cultivating resilience, and maintaining a positive mindset, individuals can increase their likelihood of success, regardless of external factors.

Base your monetary future on luck (as we have defined it in this chapter) and you will become as lucky as you want to be. Amazingly, it works!

Luck is where planning meets opportunity – become lucky!

I am a great believer in luck and I find the harder I work the more I have of it.——— Stephen Leacock

5. Time

Every successful businessperson, when planning for the future, takes stock of business assets and available resources. You have already looked at your assets and, in particular, the greatest asset of all – your brain. I trust that by now you believe in yourself, your greatest asset, and that you have faith in what that asset will do for you.

So now let us concentrate on resources and on the greatest resource of all. This is a bank account that we all have in common, but a bank account with peculiarities: you cannot invest into this account, make a deposit or obtain a statement – all you can do is withdraw. It is the bank account of time. Every day, we take another day out of this bank account, yet this valuable resource cannot be replaced. It is tragic that so many people take their time for granted and undervalue each day. It only takes a visit to a hospice to spend time with people who are terminally ill to truly understand the value of time and of using it well.

WORK, REST AND PLAY

If we are really fortunate, our time is divided in three ways: a third of our life at work; a third at play (evenings, weekends, holidays and retirement); and a third asleep.

Work time and play time

If people are happy at work, they are generally more happy at play and vice versa. I believe that if people are unhappy in their private lives it can affect their performance and, of course, success at work.

As I understand it, the primary reason for going to work is to earn some money. Why do we want the money? To pay for our play time. Now I call this one incident with one of my friend who was working as a Web developer said, 'I must disagree with that – I love my job.' I did not contradict, but shared that interesting thought with one of my diplomatic friend, who in contradiction said, 'Would you still go to work if you weren't being paid?' You can imagine the reply.

Of course, it is quite true that we go to work for lots of reasons, and the greatest motivator in the world for all of us is to do something we enjoy. If we can achieve this during work time, fantastic.

STRESS

The last few years has seen stress become a major concern in the business arena. More and more courses on how to manage stress are appearing. Thousands of corporations employ stress consultants. Vast sums of money are being expended on learning how to cope with stress, stress counselling and dealing with the results of stress. But it seems that very little effort or thought is being directed at the cause or the prevention.

My personal opinion is that stress is good, as long as it is managed. Stress, in some cases, results in better performance. Adrenalin can raise levels of achievement, but stress must be managed and prevented from causing a medical condition, which can be extremely serious. Doctors' surgeries are full of people suffering from stress, unhappiness, pressure and relationship problems.

The causes of stress

The biggest cause of stress at work is the mismanagement of time: people taking bulging briefcases home, not opening them, taking the same briefcase back to work and then feeling guilty. Piles of paperwork build up without action or decisions being taken. The second biggest cause of stress is very simple: lack of training, or the 'square peg in a round hole' scenario. People who are put into jobs for which they have not been trained, or for which they are not qualified, become unable to cope. They then experience dramatic loss of confidence and feel terribly stressed due to the expectations of others and their inability to live up to the expectations of others – and still they receive no training.

Many people get promoted because they demonstrate skills or perform well in another arena and are then expected to be able to manage, lead and motivate, without being trained in how to do so. The third cause of stress is sheer work overload with appraisal only once a year. Of course, another great source of stress, which has become more and more common, is the threat of redundancy.

Preventing stress

In the vast majority of cases, stress can so easily be prevented by training and by individuals personally developing themselves. But we still live in an environment where the majority of people spend very little money or time on their own personal development, and if their employers do not provide facilities or they are not available elsewhere, they never get the opportunity. Although stress can be a useful motivator, it requires management through the effective use of time, learning, personal development and prioritizing.

Activity and Achievement

There is a great difference between activity and achievement. Think of a time when you were busy all day but felt that you hadn't actually achieved anything, despite feeling as if you hadn't stopped. I suggest that when you go home you do not feel as good, as positive or even as relaxed – it has been 'one of those days'.

Now think of another day when you have also been busy, but it has been a day of achievement. You did that awful job you had been putting off for a while, you finished that report, you won some new business and it was a real day of progress and achievement. How did you feel that evening? Of course it will be a much more enjoyable evening and your play time will be more fulfilling.

So, how can you make every day a day of achievement rather than a day of activity? The very simple concept of time management has never really been improved upon, yet a whole industry grew out of the original idea: Filofaxes, personal organizers, palmtops, and numerous time management systems and planners. Many of them have complicated the simplicity of the original idea, but nevertheless will be very effective for you.

A simple time-management system

We all have the same 24 hours in every day, which breaks down to 86,400 seconds. The busiest people in the world – prime ministers and presidents, entrepreneurs, athletes, entertainers and business leaders – still have only 86,400 seconds in their day. They may have less play time than achievement time – in other words, they work longer hours – but they still have the same hours in the day as you and I.

If you really want to get more done in a day, try using the following system.

First, at the end of a day, just before you leave the office or finish your work for the day, draw up a list of the most important jobs to do the next day. This list can be in a diary, or even on a sheet of paper. It does not really matter what you call it – 'to do list' or the 'today list' – just do it at the end of the day. Secondly, number that list of tasks in their order of importance. Finally, the following day when you decide to start work, start at number one and keep on until it is complete and then progress to number two, and so on until you have worked your way through the list.

So why is the above system so effective? Let us see.

Making the system work

1. Compile lists the night before

This is the reverse of what so many of us used to do, ie prepare our plan for the day first thing in the morning. The problem with that was that while you were deciding on the activities for the day, the phone would ring, e-mails would arrive and people would come in with their own priorities, and before you knew it, the day would be out of control and you became reactive rather than proactive. Also, the brain is most effective in the early part of the day, so why waste energy making up your mind what to do, when you could be getting on and doing it?

2. . During the day, tick off the items

Ticking off completed tasks is highly motivational as you can see yourself progressing. So you will be managing your greatest asset, your brain, and be helping it to be more motivated and to perform more effectively.

3. Adhere to your list

Most days the list will not be completed, but if you adhere to it, the tasks that you concentrate on and complete will be the most important.

4. Prioritize and do the nasty job first

The number one of most lists is nearly always the most unpleasant. There is the temptation to do the quick and easy tasks first and then get round to the longer or more unpleasant jobs. You cannot kid yourself: if you know you have to do a rotten job, but you do the quick and easy ones instead, you never do them as well, as effectively or even as speedily because you know that rotten job is lurking in the background. On the other hand, when you have completed a rotten job, how do you feel? Relieved, elated and more motivated. Manage your assets and resources – it is amazing what can be achieved.

5. Deal with interruptions effectively

Finally, be realistic. Do you ever have a day when you can crack on with your list without interruption? I do not think I have ever had one. So how do you handle the interruptions, the phone calls, the emergency, the crisis or somebody else's demands? I have found the following to be most effective. Ask yourself: Is this more important than what I am doing now, yes or no? If it is more important, deal with it immediately, and if it is not, add it to the list somewhere.

You may be thinking: Well, that's all very well, but how do I make that decision?

Let me pass on a system of prioritization that I have found to be very effective in business. The number one priority is anything that earns revenue. It might be handling a customer complaint, it might be the dispatch, it might be the chance of an extra sale or business, but the number one priority must be revenue coming in. With that as a priority, yours and everybody else's future is more secure.

The second priority when faced with an interruption is helping somebody else. It may be a decision that has to be made, it may be some guidance or training or support. It may be a response to a memo or correspondence. T

he third priority is dealing with problems, and it is very interesting that if the first two are operational, there are fewer of number three

Procrastination

Procrastination (ie putting off things that need to be done) has to be beaten if you are going to achieve success. A procrastinator might say:

○ 'Now is not the right time.'
○ 'I'll get around to it.'
○ 'The conditions aren't perfect at the moment.'

Do you imagine that successful people allow themselves to procrastinate? Of course not, but it is an absolute guaranteed characteristic of the non-achievers, or those who are dissatisfied. Try using three little words that can be a powerful self-motivator: **DO IT NOW**.

Try not to waste your time; utilize every waking minute of the day. In addition, do not let other people waste your valuable time. Virtually every successful person, I am sure, would agree that they cannot abide time wasters. Make sure that the finite amount of time we have available, 'our bank account', is not pilfered by others, or indeed by yourself.

6. Self- Management

In order to succeed, any major project needs a process of management. So it is with your project to be successful. The project needs to be managed properly and the only person who can do that is you.

This chapter is about self-management. Self-management is a positive activity and you should be able to embrace the idea more enthusiastically than self-control or self-discipline.

MANAGING YOURSELF

Everybody is a manager. Some people have the responsibility of managing others as well as themselves, but I earnestly believe that in order to be an effective leader or manager of others, one has to master self-management first. I cannot think of any person who has achieved great success in any given field, be it in business, sport, entertainment or politics, who has not exhibited self-control, self-discipline and self-management. Sadly, prisons throughout the world contain many people who were unable to resist the negative temptations of the world and lacked self-control. Selfcontrol is perhaps best described as thought control, and it is from this stance that we should approach the amazing opportunities that self-management can create for us as we progress towards success and happiness.

Imagine that you have with you at all times – like some head of state – two advisers. Like political advisers they are faceless and invisible, yet you can hear their advice on everything you plan to do. We will call these advisers Mr Success and Mr Failure. They work 24 hours a day, and the harder they work, the more persistent they become with their suggestions. These two can totally influence the results and achievement in your life. Ask yourself, who have you been taking advice from for most of your life so far?

Imagine a cold winter's morning. The alarm clock goes off. Mr Success always calls this your 'opportunity clock' because it heralds another day of opportunities to be successful. Mr Failure still calls it an 'alarm clock' as he fears the coming of a new day. Mr Success motivates you by saying, 'Great – another day, let's get cracking', while Mr Failure says, 'Bury the clock, stay in bed for another threequarters of an hour, it's nice and cosy and warm and you don't really want to get going so early.'

Now, if Mr Failure has been running your life and thoughts for years, you stay in bed, and more than likely Mr Success's enthusiasm for achievement does not even enter your mind.

SELF-MANAGEMENT TECHNIQUES

So how can we get Mr Success to work for us? Because as hard as we try, we cannot fire Mr Failure. I have tried and he is always there at some stage or other to find a weakness. All we can do is to try to keep him on sick leave. The way to develop Mr Success's muscle power and endless determination and enthusiasm will be by providing him with a burning goal (refer also to Chapter 7 – Goals: The Purpose of Life). Self-management, self-discipline and selfcontrol become automatic when we have goals. If the goal is realistic, if it is valid, if we want it far more than anything else, our thought processes and behavioural patterns really do become automatic.

Changing bad habits and routines

Now let us develop these ideas into real practicality. So much of Mr Failure's strength is due to bad habits. In order to change our habits or performance, we must change the patterns or routines behind them. In order to change the result, we must change our patterns and routines. Consider the simplest and easiest way for a smoker to give up smoking. The stages are incredibly simple:

- Stage one – really decide to stop. You cannot stop if you do not want to.

- Stage two – break the pattern, change the routine.

During the first two or three days, you may crave a cigarette from time to time. That actual craving only lasts for 10–20 seconds and you will get a message from Mr Failure: 'I want a cigarette.' Just say to yourself, I am a non-smoker, I do not want one, and the craving speedily disappears. Obviously, it will be harder if you are mixing with people who are continually lighting up around you.

The real test is when you return from holiday to the old routine. After two weeks without cigarettes, the craving will have dramatically diminished, with the temptation lasting only a few seconds at a time, so you will have broken out of your original pattern and routine. A great definition of stupidity is to do the same thing next year as you have done this year and expect a different result.

Admit your weakness

Every one of us has strengths and weaknesses. I am convinced that there is real strength in admitting to and being honest about one's weaknesses. I understand from people who work with alcoholics that treatment can start only when a person is able to admit he or she is an alcoholic. It takes strength and courage to seek help, but the goal of being non-dependent upon alcohol is far more important than Mr Failure urging you to 'have one more drink, it won't do any harm, and why shouldn't you anyhow?'

TEN STEPS TO MASTER SELF-MANAGEMENT

Changing bad habits/routines and admitting your weaknesses are the foundation blocks of self-management, so let us run through 10 stages to effectively reinforce these principles.

1.Control what you say and how you say it

Control what you say – manage the words that come out of your mouth. It is a well-known fact that it is more profitable for us all as individuals to listen than speak (after all, we have two ears and one mouth). Also remember that it is rude to talk at or over the top of other people's conversation. So, you must be able to decide when it is right to keep quiet and listen and when to assert your point of view. Maintaining a balance is the key to fluent conversation, but if this is too hard, keep quiet.

It is a characteristic of the most successful and popular people that they appear to be naturally good listeners. It is self-management – they have achieved a balance between talking and listening.

2. Do not lose self-control

The loss of self-control immediately gives an advantage to other people. Many people waste an enormous amount of power and energy by retaliating through anger, or trying to get their own back.

Ensure your facial expression always has an element of a smile or concentration. If you never show anger, temper or loss of control, you will always maintain credibility, as well as controlling the situation. Lose your temper and you've lost.

So, use your brain and remember, it does not matter what anybody else says, thinks or does – it is what you do that matters.

3. Do the nasty job first

Another tip that I have found useful over the years is to always do the nasty job first. It requires self-discipline, but it is so easy. Mr Failure says, 'Do it later on, get around to doing it, do something more enjoyable.' Mr Success: 'Do it now, get it done and you'll be so pleased once it's been tackled.' Like all good habits, it takes a little while to acquire, but it will soon become automatic.

> This is probably the major characteristic of the high achiever – the willingness to tackle the nasty job first. If there is only one piece of advice that you take from this book, take this one – it will reap you untold rewards from less stress to greater respect, from low achievement to high achievement, from weak self-management to self-control, from being unlucky to being lucky.

4. Reward yourself

Having done something nasty or unpleasant, give yourself something to look forward to. Many of us, as children, were promised a sweet by our parents after a dose of disgusting medicine. Do the same thing for yourself: it gives you an incentive to finish the nasty job and move on (after your reward, of course).

5.Use a time-management system

Mr Failure will encourage you to ignore this. Ask yourself right now: in all honesty, are you using your time as effectively as it could be used? If the answer is negative, Mr Failure is influencing your self-management.

6. Handle procrastination and temptation

Procrastination is putting off getting round to something that one should be doing. I have already suggested that no successful person in any sphere exhibits a high level of procrastination. Procrastination and achievement find it impossible to work together. Those three little words DO IT NOW are a great self-motivator. Remember the saying 'Don't put off until tomorrow what you can do today.' Put it into action yourself.

7. Goals: The Purpose of Life

You can have anything you want, but you cannot have everything.

You have only 24 hours in a day, you can only ever be in one place at one time and you have only so many years on this planet. So you literally cannot have it all, even if you were foolish enough to consider it feasible.

If you desire success, you need to have clear ambitions. The whole principle of achieving success is to translate your desires into the results that you want. This is called setting goals.

WHAT IS A GOAL?

The Oxford English Dictionary defines a goal as 'the object of a person's ambition or effort... a destination... an aim'. This is, of course, exactly the simplicity of this message.

Everyone must have an aim, a destination that one is trying to arrive at. Let me quote again that simple but truthful cliché: 'A person going nowhere gets there.'

Goals of survival and goals of achievement

Everybody has some sort of goal. Of course, there are extremes. Some people do not think beyond their next meal. For others, their goal is a drink of alcohol, and for many their goal is just to get through the day – these are goals of survival. At the other extreme are the great human achievements: the one-tenth of a second shaved off a world record, the acquisition of a multi-million-pound company, the perfection of a piece of music or work of art. Between these two extremes we find the majority of us who, unfortunately, have a poor ratio of goals of achievement as against goals of survival.

The purpose of your life is not to let the circumstances of life push and pull you. It is for you to decide what you want your life to be. This chapter will enable you to set horizons towards which you will progress. Your journey to success is towards the goals that you will set for yourself, and the fuel that will power you towards your goals is the strength of the desire that you have to achieve your success. This chapter is thus of vital importance to you in becoming as successful as you wish.

Realistic goals

Let me stress again, you can have anything you really want if you set it as your goal. Note that I have emphasized the word 'really'. We all go through life seeing and hearing of things we would like to do. We often think, 'If only I could do that', or 'If only I could have that', but ask yourself the question – is that what you really want? I could not be a dancer, nor would I want to be: I am a wee bit too old, my body is the wrong shape and anyhow, it does not motivate or inspire me, and even if it did, we have to get our ambitions into perspective – we have to be positive realists.

Although goals must be ambitious, they must also be achievable. Distinguish between the goals of achievement and the goals of survival, ie everyday activities. We invariably acquire the things we really want and we achieve the ambitions we really aspire to. The majority of your personal acquisitions have been gained because you really wanted them. The success or achievement in your life to date will have come about almost certainly because you really wanted that achievement. If that is so, then goals for the future can easily be set and the achievement of those goals will become automatic by using the techniques set out in this chapter.

Achievement through goals

Without goals, nothing can be achieved. There is not one single success story that was not goal inspired. Whether we look at sporting achievements, mountain climbing, medical research, computer technology, warfare, music, the arts or business, every achievement is goal inspired. In some cases, owing to urgency and even fear, humankind's creativity and inspiration achieves advancement that hitherto may have been beyond realistic capability.

POSITIVE GOALS

In the pursuit of success and fulfillment, the significance of setting positive goals cannot be overstated. Positive goals serve as guiding beacons, illuminating the path towards growth, achievement, and personal transformation. Unlike vague or negative goals, which may leave us feeling aimless or discouraged, positive goals empower us to channel our energy and focus towards tangible aspirations that inspire and uplift us.

Positive goals are characterized by their clarity, optimism, and alignment with our deepest values and aspirations. When we set positive goals, we cultivate a mindset of abundance and possibility, enabling us to envision a brighter future filled with opportunity and growth. Instead of dwelling on limitations or setbacks, positive goals encourage us to embrace challenges as stepping stones towards our desired outcomes.

Consider the example of a young entrepreneur who dreams of launching a successful tech startup. Rather than fixating on potential obstacles or failures, they set positive goals that reflect their vision for innovation, impact, and success. With each milestone achieved and challenge overcome, their positive goals serve as constant reminders of the incredible potential that lies within their reach.

By infusing our goals with positivity and optimism, we unleash our full potential and pave the way for extraordinary achievements. Each positive goal we set becomes a catalyst for growth, resilience, and self-discovery, propelling us towards a future defined by fulfillment, purpose, and boundless possibility.

EDUCATION AND KNOWLEDGE

Education and knowledge are the cornerstones of personal and societal advancement, serving as catalysts for growth, innovation, and empowerment. In today's rapidly evolving world, the importance of education cannot be overstated. It is the key that unlocks doors of opportunity, expands horizons, and equips individuals with the tools they need to navigate the complexities of life.

Education is not merely about acquiring information; it is about cultivating critical thinking skills, fostering creativity, and instilling a thirst for lifelong learning. Whether through formal schooling, hands-on experiences, or self-directed exploration, every encounter with knowledge enriches our understanding of the world and empowers us to make informed decisions.

Consider the example of Malala Yousafzai, the Pakistani activist for female education and the youngest Nobel Prize laureate. Despite facing adversity and violence for her advocacy, Malala remained steadfast in her belief in the transformative power of education. Her courageous efforts to promote girls' education not only sparked global awareness but also inspired countless individuals to stand up for their right to learn.

Education and knowledge empower individuals to transcend barriers, overcome challenges, and realize their full potential. They provide the foundation upon which dreams are built and futures are shaped. Whether pursuing a formal degree, mastering a trade, or simply seeking to broaden one's horizons, the pursuit of education opens doors to endless possibilities and opportunities for growth.

How important is education?

According to a survey of the top 20 most successful entrepreneurs, only 4 went to university. Two more had experienced some formal business training. The remainder went through the 'university of life', but the survey went on to report that even though some 70 per cent were not highly educated, they all regretted it. These statistics show that university education is not a prerequisite for amassing money. I am in no way deriding university education. Nevertheless, education, without question, in all its various forms, whether formal or otherwise, is not a prerequisite for success and achievement.

I once had great difficulty in accepting the following statement: 'Formal education has one purpose only in life and that is to get us our first job – self-education earns us our living.' Initially, I felt this statement was a total devaluation of everything that an education system sets out to do, but of course it is right. The school, college and university years are immensely important, but the actual knowledge gained during those years is not necessarily of use in providing students with their standard of living. It therefore becomes even more important that the knowledge and experiences gained after leaving formal education become more valuable from a monetary future viewpoint.

Applying knowledge

Once again, I must stress that it is desire that is overwhelmingly important – ability, skill or knowledge can be gained later on. Many people overestimate the power of knowledge. While essential in the academic world, in a business environment it is only potential power – we are paid for what we do with our knowledge. Many young people leaving education find this to be a dramatic setback to their beliefs and understanding. For many, their confidence and self-image has been totally dependent upon education and they have worked hard to gain qualifications that are of value in gaining interviews and obtaining jobs, but of little practical use until that knowledge can be applied practically.

THE IMPORTANCE OF SETTING GOALS

So, why is it that so few people set goals, and why is goal setting not taught at school, college and university? Why are our great seats of learning not teaching their students that they can have anything they want? This of course is an immensely complex question, and one that is beyond the remit of this book, but suffice it to say that educationalists almost certainly have not been taught the value of goal setting themselves. Generally, people do not set goals because they do not believe they can get what they want. They believe that other people can achieve their goals, but not them. This in turn produces a poor self-image, as I described earlier. If by now you accept the premise that it is desire, not ability, that determines our success, how do you build up your desire? You build desire by setting goals.

While striving towards any goal you will almost certainly encounter setbacks. There will be unforeseen circumstances and there will, of course, be days when you are tempted to say, 'Just my luck', but a person striving towards that goal transcends those setbacks and in the process builds the principles of philosophy and achievement. The setbacks in themselves are a major part of personal growth and development. We will be looking at this further in Chapters.

How to devise goals

Let us now progress to the goal-setting programme so you can decide what it is you really want, and how to build the desire, ie the energy and the fuel for achievement.

1. Goals must be ambitious but achievable :

Goals must be ambitious, but also within our reach. Everyday activities are not goals. A goal is something that you really want, but are currently not experiencing. If you do not change anything in your life you will not experience anything different.

2. Make a list of all your goals

Make a list of the things that you really want. This list should be divided into long-term and mid-term as well as short-term goals. The list can contain what some may classify as really big goals, and should include goals in your business life and your private life. Don't forget goals for personal development: hobbies, sports and social activities. These goals can be tangible, such as acquiring possessions and money, as well as intangible, like health and fitness, or the ability to inspire and communicate. This can be an enjoyable and entertaining exercise, but it is not a game – it is a deadly serious activity that is essential for success.

3. Discuss your goals with your partner

If you share your life with somebody else, this exercise must be done together. Two people with goals, some of which may be different and some of which they hold in common, become an incredibly powerful winning force. But if they have a completely separate list of goals that are not shared, this may become a recipe for conflict in the future. Partners do not have to have the same interests, hobbies, goals or ambitions, but there must be some fundamental goals that they share. This then gives each partner in that relationship understanding and respect for the other's goals and ambitions, and there is strength in that they are shared together.

4. Ensure you set your own goals

Set goals that you really want, not wishes that other people may aspire to, and do not feel pressurized by media hype. They must be your goals; it is your life. Be realistic if money is involved.

5. Set deadlines

Decide when exactly you want to achieve a certain goal. Goal setting and achievement are not effective without a timescale. The brain is not fuelled or energized, it cannot respond, without a deadline. Start off with the year, move on to the month and then to the precise date.

6. Carry your list of goals with you

Write down and carry with you this list of goals. I have found over the years that compiling a list of goals, especially for the first time, takes time. It may take several hours, even days or weeks. This does not matter, but having put the time in and having experienced the sheer excitement of concentrating on what we want to do rather than what we do not want to do, we must not waste this effort. Write that complete list down with the date alongside each goal. Some of those goals may be for 10 or 20 years hence. Some of the goals on your very first list will change with time. Many of us, at the end of a year, think about our goals for the forthcoming year. Some of these will change as the year develops, due to circumstances that may be outside our immediate control. Further guidance on this is provided at the end of the chapter.

7. Be flexible when planning your goals

Don't be afraid to adapt your goals as new information, new experiences and new knowledge come along.

8. Give up things that are barriers to your goal

Give up anything that is in direct opposition to your goal. Remember what I said in Chapter 6 – Self-management: if you have to change your patterns and routines and if you feel you are making a sacrifice, remember, it is not a sacrifice, it is a step towards your goal, which is much more important to you than whatever you are going to sacrifice. Do not, under any circumstances, allow past habits, weaknesses or procrastination to block the path to your success, achievement and happiness.

9. Be careful with whom you share your goals

By all means share with anybody what can best be described as 'give up' goals, such as losing weight, becoming fitter, or anything else that relates to personal development. But regarding goals that relate to personal advancement and acquisitions, be very careful whom you tell. There are many people who will be supportive of your attempts to become fitter or to lose weight, but who will be extremely negative towards your making more money, having a better lifestyle, driving a new car. Unfortunately, jealousy is one of the worst human characteristics. It eats away at people by generating continual negative thoughts and energy, which could otherwise be used towards achieving success and happiness.

10. Start to visualize your goals

Picture yourself actually having attained your goals we will discuss this in more detail, but please do not dismiss this stage. When I first learnt about goals, I had great difficulty imagining I had achieved them when I knew perfectly well that I had not. Keep in mind that wonderful quotation *'Whatever the mind of man can accurately conceive and believe, it is forced to achieve.'*

WRITING OUT YOUR GOALS

Take some time to write down your goals. You can use the box on the next page to make a list. Discuss your goals with your partner if you have one and distinguish between the ones you have in common and those that are personal to you. Separate your business goals from your personal goals, asking yourself, 'What do I really want?', and then be realistic, but not unambitious. Remember to put realistic dates against each goal, whether tangible or intangible.

MY GOALS
Work Personal Target Date

Long-Term:
Mid-Term:
Short-Term:

8. Personal Planning

I am sure you have heard the much-used cliché *'People don't plan to fail, they fail to plan.'*

Imagine boarding a plane for the holiday of a lifetime, filled with excitement and anticipation. As you settle into your seat, you strike up a conversation with one of the flight attendants and inquire about the flight's route and destination. To your surprise, the flight attendant responds with uncertainty, admitting that they haven't thought about the route and are unsure of the plan. They reassure you by saying, "Don't worry, I'm sure somebody else does."

Now, picture yourself in this scenario. Would you feel comfortable flying with an airline where the flight attendants are unaware of the flight plan and resources available? The lack of a detailed plan and awareness of resources could lead to disastrous consequences, similar to a ship being destroyed on a rocky coastline due to a captain's lack of planning.

Just like you wouldn't entrust your safety to a flight attendant who lacks a clear plan, why should you approach your own life any differently? Just as a well-planned flight ensures a safe and smooth journey, having clear goals, plans, and awareness of available resources in life is crucial for navigating challenges and achieving success.

The above analogy emphasizes, I hope, the importance of personal planning.

The plans and goals that you set become the purpose of your life. The stronger and more enthusiastic your desire for the goal, the more likely you are to achieve it. There is nothing wrong with that. I suggested earlier that power comes from organized energy and effort. Achieving the plan is utilizing that power within you.

PRIORITIZING

In Chapter 7 – Goals, I discussed the most effective system for planning and prioritizing the key objectives of each day. With this sort of self-discipline and planning, your life and goals become very systematic. I will state it once again: every success is the result of a plan.

Creating the master plan

So, how does one go about creating the master plan and then the detailed support plan for each goal? Well, like everything else it is incredibly simple and just downright common sense. These are the main principles:

1. Set a deadline

I stressed the importance of setting a date or deadline for each goal. Ideally, the maximum time is three months. Yes, of course you can have long-term objectives, but in order to motivate yourself, the shorter the time period, the better. A very large goal should be broken down into more easily managed, short timescales.

Imagine you are going to catch a plane next Thursday at 7 pm and today is Saturday. You may feel excited, but as far as adrenalin flow, extra effort and personal self-motivation go, the departure time is of little significance at this stage. On Thursday, the time of departure takes on a greater significance. By midday, every effort is being made to remove any barriers that might stop you getting you to the airport on time. By around about 5 pm it is all systems go. It is amazing how very few people ever miss a plane!

You must manage your most valuable asset, your brain. Set it too big a goal in too short a timeframe and the resulting non-achievement becomes a powerful negative influence, leading to disillusionment.

The importance of this message is twofold. First, aim to have a cut-off time, and secondly, remember that the greater proportion of effort is put in as the cut-off time gets closer. We are motivated when the goal is not too far away

2. Break the plan down into easily achievable stages

Another phrase that has had a direct impact on my life is the cliché *'Success by the inch is a cinch, and by the yard it is hard.'*

If someone asked you, 'Could you walk from Delhi to Shimla?', your initial response might be, 'I don't think I could manage that.' But let's reframe the question: 'Could you walk for five miles in a day?' Your answer would likely be, 'Yes, I could certainly do that.' And if you repeat this daily, in just 10 days, you would have covered the journey.

This example highlights the significance of breaking down monumental goals into manageable, achievable stages. Just as the thought of traversing the vast distance from Delhi to Shimla might seem daunting, the prospect of walking five miles in a day feels attainable. By tackling the journey in smaller increments, you can overcome any sense of overwhelm and steadily progress towards your ultimate destination.

3. Be prepared to change direction

You must be prepared to change the route or direction of your goal, if necessary. You do not have to change the goal, but the way it is achieved or planned may need on occasion to be changed owing to external influences which may be outside your control. But you must take care as this is a great opportunity for Mr Failure to find an excuse.

What I mean by external influences over which you have no control are such things as government policy, interest rate changes, redundancy, the public not buying your products as fashion changes. Such uncontrollable factors may make it necessary to change the direction of your plans.

History is full of people and organizations that through stubbornness, short-sightedness or stupidity are unwilling to change direction in order to achieve their goals. I recall a conversation with a publisher and my question was 'What business are you in?' and the reply was 'Publishing books.' My next question was 'What is your goal?' 'To publish books that people will read', he replied. 'Yes, I'm sure you're right', I said.

'But surely your business is not just the publishing of books but the selling of books, because without sales you'll have no business?'

If a company's long-term plan is to stay in business and make profits for reinvestment and security, as well as for shareholders and investors, it may have to look for new markets and new sales opportunities. Similarly, we must consider our long-term goals and be prepared to change direction if necessary.

4. Check your plan regularly to ensure you are on the right course

Most plans should be broken down into various stages, with scheduled completion dates. Are you on course or is a bit more effort required? Have you missed a deadline or are you ahead of schedule? Do check regularly where you are on your plan and, indeed, if you are still on the right course.

5. Concentrate your thoughts

Remember to concentrate your thoughts on what you want, rather than what you do not want. If you catch yourself thinking about the latter, instantaneously change that thought and replace it with what you do want.

6. Build support for your plan

If you are not receiving support from your partner, try to understand their viewpoint. This may require discussion in order to stamp out any selfish behaviour on your part. I am not saying that you should forsake your plans, but a little bit of effort to build the support and create team spirit will be well worthwhile.

7. Only ask the opinions of those who are qualified

It is perfectly normal to seek opinions or advice when attempting to solve a problem or prepare a plan of action, but be careful who you ask. If you are looking for advice or opinions, always ask yourself, 'Is this opinion really worth listening to?' Consider the experience or qualifications of the person you are asking.

8. Consider what you have to do to achieve your goal

Now create the plan. This is the most enjoyable part of the exercise. It can be a personal brainstorming session. In Chapter 2, I suggested that you ask yourself for ideas and solutions. In preparing your plan, ask yourself the key question:

'What do I have to do to achieve .... (your goal)'. The ideas then unfold. Just put them on a sheet of paper so you can prioritize them when you finalize your plan.

9. Ensure your plan is visible at all times

Ensure your goal plan is visible – at least to you. The ship's captain has a chartroom and chart table with a route plan clearly visible at all times; any pilot will be able to tell you, at any given time, exactly where they are on that plan, to within a few feet.

'The person who is sure nothing can be done is usually the person who has never done anything.'
- Bits and Pieces

9. Using Visualization

It has to be said that the satisfaction and excitement you gain from having goals and plans is that as you achieve your goals your confidence grows alongside your competence and skills and this encourages you to set even bigger goals. You know the expression 'Seeing ourselves progressing motivates us.'

VISUALIZATION TECHNIQUES

From that personal experience, I now totally understand and believe in the importance of visualizing what it is you really want, because today we talk less about goal imagination than goal visualization

Practical methods

I want to stick to ideas, systems and thoughts that I have tested and found worked for me and for countless thousands of others. Fundamentally, these principles really do not change. People may give them new names, but peel away the verbiage and the principle is the same underneath. Henry Ford, who is always held to be one of the great success stories, is quoted as saying, *'If you think you can, or you think you can't – you're right.'* That is fundamentally correct. Let me repeat, once again, the only limitations are the ones you impose on yourself.

Negative visualization

How often have you heard people say:

- 'I knew I wouldn't win.'

- 'I knew I couldn't do that.'
- 'I knew that ball would go into the bunker.'
- 'I knew I wouldn't get that job.'
- 'I knew I wouldn't get that sale.'
- 'I don't see myself winning that race.'
- 'This is going to be a bad month/week/day.'

These are just a few examples of negative visualization. Any person with these types of thought is absolutely certain to achieve that negative result. 'I knew I wouldn't' – if that thought is in the forefront of your mind, it is almost pointless to proceed, because that alone will make the goal impossible to achieve.

Positive visualization

The first time in the history of human endeavour that the power of visualization was fully exemplified was in the story of Roger Bannister running a mile in under four minutes in 1954. Up until that time, nobody had ever run a mile in under four minutes. It was generally believed it could not be done. While at Oxford University, Roger Bannister had run a quarter of a mile in under a minute on numerous occasions and he visualized putting together these four quarters and running a mile in under four minutes. Well, we all know the result. What was so amazing about that achievement was that his body had not changed, and there were no new running tracks or track shoes. His mindset, his belief and his visualization had most certainly changed. I am sure he knew he was going to break the four-minute mile record.

If he can – I can

Interestingly, within days, people were running the mile in under four minutes, because Roger Bannister had given them the chance to believe they could. The 'If he can, I can' attitude was exemplified. He visualized and the followers after that first epic event did not have to use their imagination. Their mindset had gone through a dramatic change.

So, visualization can be positive as well as negative. Unfortunately, it is more commonly used negatively. How often have you found yourself worrying about things you do not want? The more you visualize the failure scenario, the more certain it is that this is the scenario which will come about. There is that well-known saying 'What you fear may come upon you.'

Positive, creative visualization is one of the stages in your success plan and this entails consciously maintaining the image of what you want to achieve.

Throughout our lives, we unconsciously use visualization. Virtually everything we do and achieve, we have thought about beforehand. To achieve your success, you must wilfully and determinedly switch negative visualization into positive visualization.

Active positive visualization

If you catch yourself thinking, worrying or seeing yourself in a situation that you do not want to be in, immediately replace that thought with a situation that you do want to be in. The brain visualizes pictures rather than words. Of course, we communicate with words, but these are instantaneously transposed into pictorial images in our mind. In Chapter 3 – Believe in Yourself, I discussed self-image: people who succeed have a great self-image and people who fail have a miserable self-image. If you can vividly see yourself having achieved your goal, it will become a reality.

Steve Redgrave is an awesome example of human endeavour – the greatest Olympian Britain has ever produced, the only athlete to have won gold medals at five consecutive Olympic Games. His vision, as with all winners, was paramount. He alone believed he could.

Muhammad Ali is another of the world's all-time great sportspeople. He lost only two fights in the whole of his professional boxing career and will remain in history as possibly the greatest boxer of all time. He told how having met his opponent, he would spend time in uninterrupted thought to concentrate on the forthcoming fight until he could clearly see in his mind himself winning. He visualized the result. He would then hold a press conference and announce in verse which round he would win in, and he was invariably right. He never once in his career said, 'I am going to be the greatest'; he only ever said, 'I am the greatest'.

Affirmations

If using self-image and visualization are so important, how do we continually use this knowledge positively and effectively? The answer has already been disclosed through affirmations. Most affirmations begin with 'I am...', and if from today you are sufficiently strong-willed never to make another negative affirmation to yourself, the results will, I promise you, be amazing.

If this is the very first time you have encountered these ideas, you cannot help but be sceptical. The subconscious mind needs to be fed the right information. Imagine a vast oak tree; you can see the trunk, branches and leaves, but holding up that tree is an incredible root system that could travel for 30 or 40 yards. Another analogy would be an iceberg: only a tiny proportion is visible compared to the mass that is below sealevel. It is our subconscious that programs us; it moves our muscles when we walk, turns us over in bed, influences almost every single bodily function. So, every experience is recorded in our subconscious ready for use at a later stage.

Many of us have difficulty remembering names. We may know the name, but have difficulty in the recall. This is compounded when we say, 'I'm just bad at remembering' or 'I can't remember'. So this is why it is so important to consistently and consciously think, talk and visualize your success – so that it is totally implanted into your subconscious. Equally, you will find how miraculous the subconscious can be in solving problems or overcoming difficulties.

You do not even have to say these affirmations aloud. Give your brain positive affirmations as you are going to sleep and it will store these messsages in the subconscious. Positive affirmations should be your first thought in the morning: repeat them several times a day. Let me state once again, you owe it to yourself to gradually tip the balance from the negative to the positive, until such time as the negative becomes a rarity.

Just one cautionary statement: affirmations must be positive statements of the present: 'I am successful', 'I am happy', never 'I want to be happy' or, even worse, 'I am going to be happy'.

Sporting analogies are useful in illustrating messages of personal development. With the amazing rewards available for outstanding performance, coaches and athletes seek, then test, every single idea and process that might help them to win. Hardly a week goes by without some new record being shattered. I accept that people train harder and longer and that in team sports, new skills are developed and matchplay tactics are skilfully practised and planned. The will to win is enhanced by the desire for the rich rewards of goal achievement.

This cannot be explained away by the evolution of the human body, but I am sure it can be accepted as reality by the development of the human brain in the way that people think.

Scientific research has shown that when we visualize ourselves carrying out a specific activity our brain programs alter as if we were actively performing. There are electrochemical changes in the cells which produce new behaviour.

Mental rehearsals

I have found that the more I mentally rehearse in total concentration, closing my eyes and visualizing the perfect result, the better the activity is when performed. One of the fastest ways to improve anything in our lives is to join together physical and mental activity and then to practise consistently. A very good example of this is in the work of actors and actresses. They not only learn the words, but also mentally rehearse the character. They see themselves in their parts and use their imagination to allow themselves to be what many of us would describe .

10. The Success Attitude

All the successful people I have seen over the years have one thing in common: a 'success attitude'.

This topic is worth considering because whatever sphere of activity successful people operate in, they all seem to have this common trait.

N. R. Narayana Murthy (Infosys), Mukesh Ambani (Reliance Industries), and Ratan Tata (Tata Group) are all self-made multimillionaires of the 21st century. The one thing they and all the other successful entrepreneurs have in common is a success attitude. They didn't acquire this once they had achieved their monetary wealth.

All outstanding athletes, musicians, singers and entertainers also exhibit a success attitude, as do the self-made millionaires and billionaires throughout history, and I do not believe that any of them acquired their success attitude after they achieved success.

It really is almost the only thing they have in common. So, what is the vital ingredient of your own success attitude? Of course, it is a positive outlook or attitude.

Positive attitude

It is all very well saying we have to be positive. I am certain every one of us agrees that it is essential, but what is a positive attitude? How can I get it? If I have got it, how can I keep it? Once again I thought it helpful to refer to the Oxford English Dictionary in attempting to define what a positive attitude really is: 'Constructive; directional. Marked by the presence, rather than the absence, of qualities. Tending in a direction, naturally or arbitrarily taken as that of increase or progress... (of a person) convinced, confident.'

To sum all this up and put it into a simple and memorable form, the success attitude is expressed by a mind that is purposeful, that is expecting the best, is realistically optimistic and is cheerful.

A success attitude creates success and is most certainly acquired before the success has been achieved. At the beginning of this book, I linked happiness to success. We need to draw a distinction between pleasure and happiness. Pleasure is an experience of enjoyment that one has at any given time, but does not really have any long-lasting effect. We get pleasure from hobbies, music, playing a sport, enjoying a meal, a beautiful sunset or the smell of flowers – the list is endless. These are the pleasures of life which one strives to enjoy – and, combined together, they can create happiness.

Make yourself happy

Linking happiness and success together in developing the success attitude should, of course, be your main goal. Who decides whether you are going to be happy or unhappy?

Are you dependent upon the morning news as to whether you are going to be happy or unhappy that day? Are you dependent upon the government, or the weather, or your partner or what arrives in the post?

Robin Sharma said most people are about as happy as they make up their minds to be. You and I know that we can be in control of our minds if we want to be.

Truth and honesty

I have found that people who are honest with themselves are automatically able to be honest with their fellows. In almost every single situation, our happiness is dependent on our relationships with others.

The more effective and better our communication, the greater the trust and respect we receive and the greater the happiness we can achieve. People who are not honest with others experience stress and have low self-esteem. They are nearly always non-achievers. So much time is wasted covering up a lie or remembering what one said last time.

From a communication point of view, the truth may be hard to say at times, but my goodness it is easy to remember, and it is so much nicer to deal with people who are honest.

Moral courage

Telling the truth takes moral courage, and it is great to see people who have it. You always know where you are with that person and you know you can trust them. We sometimes call this 'strength of personality'.

It is equally important not to exaggerate. I find it so frustrating that some people will exaggerate either to impress or to make a story that's anyway good even more of an attention grabber. In business and in relationships, it is so dangerous to give incorrect information. Over-exaggerated or even under-exaggerated information can prompt others to make entirely the wrong decisions.

Try asking yourself that question, and also think about the following: 'What sort of parent would you like to have?', 'What sort of brother or sister would you like to have?', 'What sort of partner would you like to have?', 'What sort of boyfriend or girlfriend would you like to have?' Now ask yourself: 'AM I THAT SORT OF PERSON?'

How to build a success attitude

I keep emphasizing how important the success attitude is; so let us see how to achieve it.

1. Expect the best

This is the foundation of positive thinking. It is how you mentally approach every day, month and year. Is it with positive thoughts or negative thoughts? When you look at your post, do you expect good news or bad news? If somebody says there is an urgent phone call, is your reaction 'What's gone wrong, am I in trouble, is there a crisis?' or do you think, 'Oh good! I'm expecting some good news.' Of course, occasionally you will have a frustrating situations, you will occasionally get something in the post that can be a bit of a shock and, realistically, you will from time to time have a bad day, but these should be exceptions to the rule.

Build your 'success attitude' by always having a positive attitude: expect good news, expect each day to be a wonderful, fun day. It is truly amazing how the interruptions to your enjoyment become fewer and fewer.

2. Make it a habit to be positive

Most habits take a little while to cultivate and transform into subconscious, automatic behaviour. Normally, when we talk about a habit, it is in a negative context: the habits of smoking, drinking, biting one's nails, etc. There are other habits that relate to thought and communication, such as:

- 'I make it a habit not to smile.'
- 'I make it a habit not to show my emotions.'
- 'I can't stop myself worrying, I'm always expecting the worst.'

These are all examples of activity and thought made into a habit by repetition. So, how about making it a habit to be positive, to be happy, to enjoy every day, and how about making it a habit to avoid some of the negative thoughts that damage your own self-image?

3. Use repetition to change your attitude

If you accept that you can be habitually positive, that will be the end result. To achieve that, you must actively use the principle of repetition. Athletes build muscle by continuous repetition. The strongest men in the world have built phenomenal strength by the continuous development of their muscles. Every day, they spend long hours repetitively pumping their muscles into and then beyond the pain threshold. Although the brain is not a muscle, it will respond like a muscle to repetition.

I have already given numerous examples of the importance of continuously giving the right messages to the brain. I believe that 10 repetitions of a thought will create the foundation upon which the skyscraper of positivity will stand.

I believe we can all change our attitudes as long as we understand what attitude is and can distinguish between positive and negative thought patterns. To those who claim attitudes cannot be changed, I reply that I have seen over the years the most wonderful achievements made by people who have changed from having a negative to having a positive attitude, a change brought on by simply being exposed to the messages I have included in this book. Nobody is born into this world negative; we are born with a positive attitude, but are conditioned to be negative.

4. Smile

Make it a habit to smile – this is probably terribly corny and rather basic, but you will find it so much harder to have negative thoughts when you are smiling. If you consciously change your facial expression, somehow the movement of muscles into a smile reflects back into the brain, and negative thoughts can seem to be replaced by something much more positive.

Smile as you wake in the morning – if you share your bed with anybody else, you will be amazed by the response! Smile as you go to work – people may look away initially, but it is so infectious that they will not be able to resist the temptation to have another look at a smiling face. Smile at your colleagues. Think how much nicer it is to talk to or be in the company of a person with a smiling and happy face.

5. Try not to burden other people

Of course, we all share some of our burdens or worries with those we are close to. Occasionally, sharing a problem with somebody else can lessen the pressure. A joy that is shared is a joy that is doubled; a problem that is shared can be a problem halved.

6. Plan on doing something positive each day

'Positive actions equal positive results.' That principle obviously leads to positive thought. But by planning and doing something each day that is constructive, you will progress towards your goal. One of the laws of motivation states that seeing ourselves progressing motivates us. Again, a motivated brain is positive and exhibits the 'success attitude'.

7. Be honest

By being honest with other people and with yourself, you will become more self-assured and more confident. Honesty with yourself allows you to know where you are and what you believe. Honesty with others enables them to know where you and they stand.

8. Discard negative

thoughts If happiness is determined by your mental outlook, it therefore seems vital to discard thoughts that make you unhappy. Easily done, first by simply determining not to think in this way, and secondly, by replacing those negative thoughts with positive thoughts.

9. Think of 'problems' as challenges

How about a life with no more problems? I have asked this question to many of my friends and have always had an enthusiastic, positive response: 'Oh, wouldn't life be so much better without problems.' Well, there is one place where I can guarantee that the residents have no problems and that, of course, is the graveyard. If that is so, problems must be a hazard of life. Could it be possible, then, that the more alive and active we are, the more problems we encounter? If so, try to avoid using the word 'problem' and endeavour to call it a 'challenge'. Yes, of course it sounds a little bit simple and it may not make the situation go away, but your mind positively embraces a 'challenge', whereas a problem is such a demotivator.

In Chinese, the word *wei-chi*, literally translated, means 'crisis' and 'danger'. The same characters together also mean 'opportunity'.

10. Managing change

More change has taken place in the last 40 years than in the whole history of humankind. For your lifetime and mine, change will be with us. You can view it as a threat or an opportunity, but you cannot stop it. It is no good hoping it will go away, or nostalgically looking back wishing to bring back the 'good ol' days'. Most change actually turns out positively, but we fear change because it brings uncertainty. Are we going to be worse off? Can we meet this new challenge or expectation? Will we be able to cope? Your brain is fantastic and it will and it can. Give it the chance. Thousands, possibly millions, of people in the 1990s learnt how to use a computer for the first time. So embrace change positively, enthusiastically; see what might be and not what was.

As a final thought, accept the saying '*I can alter my life by altering the attitude of my mind.*'

Kind words can be short and easy to speak, but their echoes are truly endless.
   -Mother Theresa

11. Overcoming Setbacks

It is all very well being positive, but we also need to be realistic. Life is not one straightforward steady climb to a pinnacle of success. We all have our ups and downs, our pleasures and sorrows, our successes and failures. Most of us are extremely able to cope when things are going well, when there are no problems at home, when all is well at work, the bills are being paid, the bank is happy and goals are steadily being achieved.

Most of us do not have to learn how to cope with the successes of life, although there are situations when people achieve dramatic success and this does indeed change their behaviour. There are occasions when people have to learn how to cope with sudden or dramatic success. The consequences if they do not may mean that they are ostracized by their immediate family connections and friends, and this of course is sad and unnecessary..

This chapter is about how to manage the times of crisis, disaster or failure as well as setbacks, fears, worries and anything else that can be a barrier to our success.

We are able to manage and then overcome those downturns in order to be able to be a true positive thinker and to be able to master life with all the opportunities and joys that are available. Everybody, whoever they are, whatever they have done and achieved, has experienced and will experience from time to time a fear, a worry or a setback. The only place where one does not have a fear or a worry to cope with is a graveyard.

DEMOTIVATORS

These setbacks, fears and worries are, in most cases, demotivators and it makes sense to try to prevent ourselves from becoming demotivated. What causes you to be demotivated? Having clearly identified the causes, it is logical to do everything you possibly can to gradually eliminate them. Note that the demotivators are separate from our fears and worries and setbacks.

If you are demotivated, or your attitude is in a rut, you will be unable to make the right decisions or exert influence over others. The only difference between a rut and a grave is how long you keep working at it!

We will start by examining some of the emotions which can be barriers to our success, then we will look at how to handle them positively and overcome them.

CAUSES OF UNHAPPINESS

Prior to looking at how we can build and maintain the 'success attitude', let's examine a few human characteristics that make people feel unhappy. Unhappiness, of course, can lead to depression and it is a bit like a barometer – when it falls, stormy conditions can be expected.

Envy

Envy destroys the human heart and soul, and most who suffer from it are unaware of the destructive misery it creates not only for themselves, but also for others. In the end, envy will lead to loneliness as other people can never share their joys, successes or happiness with an envious person. In addition, an envious person uses up so much of their mental energy in negative, destructive thought, denigrating other people's achievements as dishonest, harmful or detrimental.

Bitterness and revenge

Bitterness and revenge are, of course, two different emotions, but nevertheless, one seems to feed the other in many instances. Both of these characteristics, in so many cases, deal with past events. Unfortunate past events should be left in the history books rather than be allowed to cause mental turmoil and negative thoughts. If it is consigned to the history book, we can do absolutely nothing about it, other than learn from the experience to avoid making the same mistakes again.

Revenge is wasteful as it can use up productive and creative thought. If that same creative energy and time were directed positively, the outcome would be success. If everybody followed the doctrine of an eye for an eye, the world would eventually become blind. This may sound rather pious and there are, of course, times when it is very difficult and maybe even wrong to turn the other cheek. What I am stressing is that we cannot be successful if our minds are twisted with bitterness and revenge.

Depression

Mild depression is in most cases within one's control. I mentioned it briefly in Chapter 10 – The Success Attitude, but it is worth reiterating that we cannot possibly be successful if we are suffering from depression. The causes can be so varied, and those who truly want to manage this condition will be well advised to begin by seeking the cause, the spark that lights this unfortunate fire, and then systematically taking steps to make sure that the spark is not lit: in other words, ruthlessly preventing the situations that cause depressed feelings. Regular exercise has proved to be one of the best antidotes to depression. A good walk, workout in the gym, bike ride or swim is so effective. More serious depression, of course, requires expert medical treatment and counselling, and in these cases it is no good telling a depressed person to 'snap out of it'

Bereavement

We all accept that the loss of a loved one is a cause of great unhappiness and I am not going to be so facetious or disrespectful as to suggest some glib, instantaneous technique for turning this situation into a happy experience. The success attitude is no defence to experiencing sadness as well as joy and pleasure.

If one does lose a loved one, through either death or the breakdown of a relationship, time, as we are always told, is a great healer. I can guarantee that you must have faith. But equally, it is not right to allow ourselves to wallow in our misery to such an extent that we make other people miserable. It takes positive effort and determination to stop thinking about something one can no longer do anything about and to turn our thoughts to the future. With a determined effort, try to make other people happy and, in turn, the burden will become a little lighter.

Crime and guilt

Our prisons and places of confinement are inhabited by people who have committed offences against society. These institutions are not happy places. The vast majority of the inmates, through lack of self-management, control or willpower, had believed that by taking the risk and committing a crime against society, they would somehow achieve happiness by their actions. Sadly, the opposite is true. Whatever the crime that may have been committed, the biggest theft of all is from themselves: their liberty and their life. There can be very little pleasure in gains made by unsociable behaviour. People who commit crime are generally unhappy, and even those who are not institutionalized have to live with the fear that one day their activities will be discovered. They are also ensnared by their own poor selfimage and guilt.

Family problems

If you are fortunate enough to be part of a family, of course you are going to face difficult situations, challenges and opportunities. If approached with love, care and responsibility, and without any selfish thought or action, families can bring great joy and security. The penultimate chapter of this book will deal in more detail with the great joy and happiness that is available for any of us fortunate enough to share our lives with another person.

Our own unhappiness

If we think about ourselves in a negative, dissatisfied way, of course we become unhappy. If we look at ourselves in the mirror and we are dreadfully unhappy with what we see, if our thought processes are continually self-destructive and we do not see the goodness within ourselves, unhappiness and dissatisfaction are unavoidable. You need, if you are at all unhappy, to concentrate on your positive attributes and to dedicate your energies to actively building a 'success attitude'.

OVERCOMING SETBACKS

'Prevention is better than cure': but anybody who does anything in the world experiences setbacks, and the more things you do, the more likely it is that you will experience setbacks.

Mistakes

Some people are so fearful of making a mistake that they do nothing, or try nothing new, and the consequence is that they achieve very little. It is perfectly acceptable to make mistakes occasionally – it is a sign of activity. We all learn more from our mistakes than from our achievements.

But it is very stupid to continue making the same mistake over and over again. Setbacks can be the result of a mistake, or they can be the result of situations that we find ourselves in, perhaps even through no fault of our own.

Turn setbacks to your advantage

So, whenever you are faced with those hurdles or barriers, setbacks or crises, say to yourself, 'How can I turn this to my advantage?' Just asking yourself that one question will switch your thought processes from negative to positive.

Throughout this book, the concepts and ideas for achievement and success revolve around our thought processes. It is quite extraordinary in the world, how when the world's leaders are in positive thought mode, economies grow, jobs are created and the threat of world conflict is reduced.

Natalie du Toit, the South African paralympic swimmer who won four gold medals at Athens in 2004, was knocked off her scooter when returning from training in February 2001. Her left leg was amputated just below the knee and her Olympic dream was over. She switched her attention to the Athens Paralympics. She says, 'I'm one of those people who can truthfully say, out of something bad came something good. The tragedy of life doesn't lie in not reaching your goal, the tragedy lies in having no goal to reach.' She goes on to say, *It isn't a calamity to die with dreams unfulfilled but it is a calamity not to dream. It isn't a disgrace not to reach the stars, but it is a disgrace to have no stars to reach for.*

SITUATIONS AND CHALLENGES

'Problem' is such a negative word. If you tell yourself you have a problem, you normally dwell on it and worry about it. If, instead, you delete the word 'problem' from your vocabulary and use the words 'situation' or 'challenge', your brain will respond more effectively. It becomes creative and proactive and, furthermore, you are on your way to overcoming the situation. Remember the old cliché 'When the going gets tough, the tough get going.'

Having a system or methodology for handling setbacks, only allowing yourself a short period to worry before looking for solutions, allows you to take positive action and turn it to your advantage.

OVERCOMING FEARS

There are some things it is perfectly rational to fear – drugs, drinking poison, falling over a cliff – situations in which your body is in imminent danger, but these are not the fears that we need to concentrate on overcoming. What are you afraid of? This is very personal as one person's fear is not necessarily another's. Realistically, everybody is afraid of something.

Managing fear

The best way of overcoming a fear is to keep doing the thing you fear to do. We all know this to be true and all it takes is that first step, that first little bit of courage. It is quite extraordinary how, once we have participated in an activity that has previously been a fear, our confidence grows and how much easier it is the next time, until what used to be a fear is just an everyday part of life. Fear is an imagination, not a reality. It is only the thought of what might happen that creates fear.

Worrying about what might happen

I find the easiest way is to imagine the worst scenario that could happen. In those circumstances, what would I do? How would I handle it? I then formulate in my mind a plan for handling the situation and, having prepared a plan of action in my mind, I can delete that worry and I do not think about it again. In most cases you will find that if you follow that simple procedure the worry will disappear as all your thought processes are concentrating on positive action. When you brainstorm ideas, you often find solutions to a worry

– this is really a 'positive thinker's' habit. But to continually visualize a worry scenario is perhaps what wyrgan means: 'to strangle, to choke until there is no life left'.

Writing down your worries

You may find it helpful to write your worries or fears down on a piece of paper. When they are written down, they never seem as bad as when you are mulling them over in your mind. There is another great little system that works well for some people – to have a 'worry box'. It is a little bit like a piggybank, and what you do as soon as you have a worry is to write it down on a piece of paper and put it in the 'worry box' and then, at the end of the month, empty it out with the family. You will find that not only have the majority somehow been solved, but many of the items have become a bit of a laugh rather than a worry.

I can assure you, it is very effective. From now on, whenever you are worried, do something. If you wish to achieve your goals, I really must stress that any time spent worrying will be an inhibitor.

Worrying achieves absolutely nothing other than depression and stress, so endeavour not to do it. So there is the message: if you have a worry, do something, take action, be positive; do not let it fester.

Failure is not in failing: it's in not trying.
-Stella James

12. Mastering Rejection

Rejection is normally expressed by a silly little word – No. Written down, it looks fairly harmless and hardly daunting, but the truth is that this simple word can stop you from achieving your goals. Unless you are truly able to deal with it, it will restrict your future progress.

OVERCOMING REJECTION

Rejection is, for many of us, difficult to overcome. When we were children, the word 'No' was used as a form of control: 'No, don't touch', 'No, don't step off the pavement', 'No, don't put your hand in the fire', and, as a result, we became more and more conditioned to the word 'No' preventing us from doing what we wanted – although it often stopped us from getting hurt.

Fear of the word 'no'

From our very early years, both our subconscious and our conscious minds process the word 'no' as a safety mechanism.

For example, a young man who wants to ask a girl for a date is so fearful that she might say 'No' that he does not even ask.

Why is it that people seeking a job are happier to apply lots of job applications in the hope of getting an interview than to pick up the phone and ask, or go and make a visit? The worst that can happen is that an employer will say, 'No, I don't have a vacancy', 'No, the time is not right' or, perhaps, 'No, you're not what we are looking for'.

There is a very common reaction among the vast majority of the population, who claim they could never be any good at selling. They feel they would be unable to cope with rejection, with somebody saying, 'No, thank you.'

Success, as I have repeatedly said, is available to you and this may mean doing things differently – grasping challenges, establishing relationships – and undoubtedly you are going to be confronted with many situations where people have a choice and they can say 'No'.

Another way of looking at the word 'no'

First, let us truly understand what 'No' means. It is not a rejection of you in 99 per cent of cases – and so what if it is anyhow?

I have personally found that the most effective way to deal with the word 'No' is to understand that 'No' is only 'No' at that point in time. It does not mean 'No' next week, next month or next year.

I can guarantee that you have purchased something, been somewhere or done something in the last few months that previously you said 'No' to. The reason is that your circumstances will have changed. You may have the funds, the opportunity, or more time, which means that you now buy or do what you had previously refused to buy or do.

Asking does not hurt

We have all overheard people saying, 'I just don't like asking people for anything.' Sometimes this is because that person fears being rejected or perhaps it is because they do not like being obligated or in debt to another person.

However, you must realize that asking will not hurt you and, equally, understand that some people just yearn to be asked. They are fearful of wanting to appear to impose, they are shy, they do not want to interfere and some, equally, are fearful of offering because they might be rejected. Most successful people ask if they want something done or they require information.

Now just suppose 50 per cent of the time you ask you get a 'No'. That means 50 per cent of the time you are going to be better off, you are going to get help and it may also help others – and, let me remind you, it is impossible not to be successful if you make others successful.

So, do not be a martyr – you cannot be successful without help from others.

Taking 'no' personally

So, do not ever take a 'no' personally, do not take it as a rejection – it is not a failure, it is just an unsatisfactory result at that particular moment.

Persistence

One of the most powerful ingredients of success is persistence. A person who is able to persist – and yes, you can too – will eventually prevail and win. It does not matter what the challenge or opportunity is. If you are prepared to keep tapping away at it, you will succeed in the end. Could you knock a six-inch nail into a seasoned piece of oak with one hit? Of course not, but a child could drive that nail in, perhaps even with a wooden hammer, with a sufficient number of taps, over a sufficient period of time. The opposite of persistence is giving up, and this appears to be the norm for many people. 'A river cuts through the rock not because it is sharp, but because of it's persitence'

Giving up

Try not to let giving up become a habit. Every invention that we now take for granted in our personal lives is the result of persistence. Edison made thousands of attempts to produce a light bulb; Fleming's discovery of penicillin was due to persistence. There are now drugs that not only control but, in some cases, cure cancer. Once again, this is due to persistence.

The list is endless, but all have been achieved through hundreds or even thousands of attempts and by getting it wrong until a solution was found. So, persistence is a winning ingredient. There is, however, a balance between knowing when to quit and when to be stubborn. You may absolutely hate your job or your environment and just stubbornly persist in being unhappy. There is a difference in being stubborn and being persistent, but most of us seem to give up too early.

The skill is to be totally honest with yourself. Being stubborn is a destructive trait and is therefore negative and normally requires little action to change. Being persistent is being positive, attempting some new action or a new approach. When you have run out of the new, or are spending too much time trying to salvage, this is the time to stop. You must have found how, when things look really extraordinarily bleak, they take a turn for the better. All successful people have experienced this – when the temptation to give up is so strong, and then suddenly everything seems to come right. I have heard people describe this as the eleventh hour principle so, once again, do not give in; you may just be experiencing the eleventh hour principle.

If you want something, whatever it may be, persist – persistence will master virtually any rejection.

Accept that there is absolutely nothing wrong in asking. If we look back at our life's experiences, the only things we truly regret are the things that we have not done, or did not ask for – we very rarely regret actions that we took. So, there is no logic in fearing rejection. It must come back to those pillars of pain and pleasure, where the pain is caused by somebody saying 'No' and this outweighs the pleasure that would result if they were to say 'Yes'.

Take the actions that I discussed earlier. I find it very helpful to say to myself, 'So what if they say no?' By mastering rejection, you will be more willing and more prepared to do the things you have feared doing, because you will feel that much stronger.

Whatever you do, do not visualize a negative result, do not visualize other people saying 'No' – reverse that picture in your mind.

Nothing in the world can take the place of persistence. Talent will not; nothing is more common than unsuccessful men with talent. Genius will not; unrewarded genius is almost a proverb. Education will not; the world is full of educated derelicts. Persistence and determination alone are omnipotent. The slogan 'press on' has solved and always will solve the problems of the human race.

-*Calvin Coolidge*

13. Negativity: The Success Destroyer

This book is all about success, but now comes the hazard warning – negativity destroys success. Ignore the message from this chapter at your peril.

The success destroyer has to be a major disease of the world today. It is a total destroyer of happiness, and actual and potential success. It is a destroyer of relationships and achievements. The disease I describe is the power of the negative and it manifests itself in negative thinking, which in turn leads to negative communication.

HOW DO WE BECOME NEGATIVE?

We were all born positive, but conditioned to be negative. We discussed in Chapter 12 – Mastering Rejection, how influential the word 'no' is in all our daily lives. Our brains store the context in which the word 'no' was used in our early years, so it almost becomes a word of fear. But 'no' is not a negative word, even though the majority of us react as if it is. So, how do we become conditioned to be negative?

If we are continually bombarded with bad news, is it any wonder that so many people are negative? Is it any wonder that so many people enjoying extraordinarily high living standards in the Western world, with so much pleasure and happiness available to them, are depressed? It is so easy to expect bad news, and to some extent it creates a thirst resulting in even more being demanded.

We all know that if the newspapers feature a dreadful murder, their sales increase. The vast majority of people in the Western world have so much to look forward to, have so much protection and care provided by the state, have so much that is good, yet they feel so short-changed by their governments. So few people are really looking forward to the future. They have become conditioned by this negative process.

THE DANGERS OF NEGATIVITY

Why is negativity so dangerous? First, because it is so difficult to get rid of and also extremely expensive, as you will see. It drags us down emotionally, physically and mentally. It is, I repeat, the single biggest destroyer of success and potential success.

Negative thinking destroys relationships, creativity and achievement and, ultimately, happiness. Perhaps even more frightening, negative thinking creates the right environment for illness to grow and prosper. We attract what we fear. The more one thinks about a potential illness, the more one concentrates one's thoughts about catching a particular disease, the more one imagines one has a serious complaint when only a minor symptom is exhibited, the more likely one will be to develop that particular form of ill health. It is common sense, but nevertheless worth stating, that the more one is a positive thinker, the more likely one is to remain healthy.

Negative thinking and communication

For many people, negative thinking and communication has become a bad habit that can even be addictive. So, what is it about negativity that is so bad? It affects what people say and think to themselves. I said earlier that the poorer a person's self-image, the more negative they are likely to be, creating a vicious circle.

The habit of negative thinking

These are some of the common phrases that people often say to themselves. To be realistic, every one of us can identify with some of these, but they are examples of the thoughts and phrases that have held us back from achieving the success that is available to us.

Negative thought is a destructive use of our creative imagination. We expect the worst or we anticipate something we don't want to happen to us. It can be the total fear of rejection that we have already discussed. We imagine somebody saying 'no' to us before we have even asked. This negative fear manifests itself after every news tragedy.

DEALING WITH NEGATIVE COMMUNICATION

This particular section is not so much about what you think as about how you process what is said to you by others and how you handle negative communication in all its forms. Let us look at the three Cs:

- Criticizing;
- Condemning; and
- Complaining.

Criticism

Of course, there has to be a place for constructive criticism, but a lot of criticism is not constructive; rather, it is destructive. None of us will ever grow and improve without some constructive help, but too much criticism is not constructive. Anyone can find fault. If only people would use their brilliant minds to solve problems and find better ways of doing things instead of saying, 'That won't work', 'That's a lousy idea', 'You can't do that', etc.

Living in a negative environment

The law of conformity states that as human beings we naturally conform to our environment, whatever that environment may be. So is it any wonder that if the environment is negative, people will become negative themselves?

Here is a challenge. See if you can draw up a list of really successful, but extremely negative people. I do not think you will run out of ink! Negative people are not the benchmark of success or happiness. When you visit cities throughout the world, you cannot help but notice statues erected to famous people, for their endeavours, achievements, creativity and courage. Have you ever seen a monument erected for a critic? Monuments are erected not to those who criticize, but to those who have been criticized.

Dealing with the past

If something has happened, it is now in the past. Do not use it as an excuse for misery and unhappiness, which, in turn, can be passed on to others. I cannot stress strongly enough the importance of positive rather than negative affirmations, and if there is only one message that you take from this book, this should be it.

TAKE PRECAUTIONS AGAINST NEGATIVITY

Let us look at some examples of how we respond to situations:

In hot countries, we take precautions to avoid being bitten by mosquitos. Why? Because it is painful and we risk catching malaria. So, we arm ourselves with an insect-killer and a mosquito net and we might take anti-malaria tablets.

Now, if you were bitten by a mosquito, this might be painful for 24 hours or so; but negative communication from one person to another may well change that person's life, and not just for 24 hours. Sometimes it can be for days, weeks, months or even a lifetime, yet we just let it happen.

Let me give you another example. Imagine you are driving your car on a lovely, hot, sunny day. All the windows and the sun roof are open and the traffic lights change to red. Cars draw up on either side of you and from one of the cars near you a passsenger bends down, collects up all the rubbish from inside their car and throws it straight in through your window: fish and chip wrappers, cigarette packets, drink cans all land in your car – what would you do?

I suggest you would be absolutely furious and you would almost certainly leap out and hand the rubbish back with at the very least the mildly sarcastic words 'Have you dropped these?'

Why is this such a useful example? We do not like people putting rubbish in our cars, but we allow them to put it in our minds. So, be careful. People with an open mind must be even more careful, as there are others intent on filling it full of garbage.

ELIMINATING YOUR NEGATIVITY

Here are a few steps to help you handle and, one hopes, eventually eliminate the success destroyer.

1. Check what you say to family, friends and colleagues

Is what you say positive or negative? If it is negative, you are almost certainly harming somebody else, unless you are sure you are being constructive. So, do not make negative or nasty comments – all you will be doing is harming somebody else. You are totally in control of your own verbal communication.

2. Check what you say to yourself

Are you saying positive or negative things to yourself? Imagine a missile being fired. The senders have control of it, and if it goes off course, they can press the self-destruct button and the missile will explode. Whenever you let negative thoughts enter your mind, it is as though you have just pressed the self-destruct button. You are in control of what you think. If you know those thoughts are self-destructive, actively change them and replace them with positive thoughts.

3. Avoid negative situations

As I have stated, the purpose of the body is to transport the brain, so why transport the brain into negative situations intentionally?

4. Give up negative thinking

For many people, negative thinking has become a habit and many are almost addicted to bad news. If they did not want it, the media would not provide it – the press could not survive if there was no market for bad news. Now, any addiction has control over us. So, test your habit or addiction and see if you can go for, say, 12 or even 24 hours without having a negative thought. If you achieve that, fantastic! Like all habits that one wishes to break, it takes time. So, give yourself 30 days of continually avoiding negative thoughts.

HANDLING NEGATIVITY IN OTHERS

Dealing with our own negativity is one thing, but we also need to deflect the negativity of others in order to preserve our own positive thoughts. So, here are a few tips on handling others' negativity.

1. Be understanding

When somebody says something negative to you, it is ridiculous and, in many cases, uncaring to respond with some glib comment. It may be somebody very close to you: a loved one, colleague, close friend or a member of your family. They may say something negative, voice a criticism or a complaint or a condemnation, but try to understand why it was said. Ask yourself why he or she said that. They may be feeling negative because they were worried, they may be fearful of certain consequences, or they may just be misinformed. If you are to be an effective communicator, you must learn to understand other people's feelings. You don't have to agree, but you can be very positive and optimistic and, one hopes, change their thoughts.

2. Mix with positive people

If you are in an environment where negative people are affecting you, pick up the phone and have a chat with your positive friends. Perhaps go and visit them, step out of that negative environment into a positive one.

3. Be prepared to walk away

If you find yourself in a negative environment, whatever the occasion, be prepared to walk away – it just takes common sense. In any situation that you do not like, remember it is your life and your brain, and negative situations or communication can play no part whatsoever in your success or happiness. Rather than being cowardice, walking away is, I believe, more like bravery. It is more cowardly to join in, be a part of and add to the negativity.

4. Be realistic

Build your own vocabulary and understanding of what is negative. Constructive criticism is not negative, so be enthusiastic about it. Remember, you are very fortunate if you receive it. Encourage others to offer constructive criticism.

5. Do not shoot the messenger

There is always the danger of becoming so ultra-positive that you don't want to hear the bad news. Some people in authority, whether in politics or business, surround themselves with 'yes' people, but we all know they do not last for long and they are never classified as successes. The messenger or the bearer of the bad news must be welcomed. No decisions can be taken that have any chance of success unless they are based on accurate and up-to-date information.

6. Do not overreact to other people's opinions

Remember, all opinions are just that – an opinion. They can be right or wrong. As we know, we all have the human characteristic of wanting or hoping for recognition in whatever form. Previously in this chapter, I used the media as an example of negative communication. Many lives are totally destroyed by what journalists write. Even if it is fictitious, the individual is often unable to protect him- or herself from the libel. I know personally of many people who are desperately hurt by what somebody may say or think about them: a word overheard in conversation, the overheard telephone call. But one must recognize that what is said may not be real feeling, but an attempt to be interesting or amusing. And even if it is a real feeling, do not let it hurt you. Build a bulletproof screen around yourself so that other people's opinions, if negative or hurtful, cannot penetrate. Visualize your plate-glass screen of protection now.

7. Have an antidote for negative comments

Picture in your mind the most negative person you know: the one who is always griping, moaning, finding fault, criticizing and complaining, or the person who just somehow seems to be happy when they are being negative or nasty about others. Next time you meet this person and you ask them how they are (which is always a dangerous thing to ask a negative person), be ready with your antidote. Their reply in its mildest form is usually something like 'Under the circumstances, things could be worse.' Quick as a flash, you say, 'Fantastic!' The look of surprise you will receive is reward in itself but, perhaps just as importantly, the conversation will dramatically change or the individual will seek solace away from you, among the other negative people.

'Why not go out on a limb? That's where all the fruit is.'
-Unknown

A Tribute to Mothers: The Unsung Heroes Behind Every Legend

In the grand tapestry of human history, there exists an unseen thread—a thread woven with love, sacrifice, and unwavering dedication. This thread binds together the stories of legends and luminaries who have left an indelible mark on the world, shaping the course of civilization and inspiring generations to come. Yet, amidst the accolades and admiration bestowed upon these towering figures, there lies a silent force, a beacon of strength and resilience—the mother.

Mothers, the nurturers of dreams, the guardians of hope, and the architects of greatness, hold a sacred place in the hearts of all who walk this earth. From the moment of conception, they embark on a journey of unparalleled devotion, dedicating themselves wholeheartedly to the well-being and success of their children. It is through their unwavering love and boundless sacrifices that the seeds of greatness are sown, nourished, and allowed to flourish.

The role of a housewife mother is often one of the most demanding and yet deeply fulfilling responsibilities a person can undertake. From the moment she wakes up until the time she rests her head at night, a housewife mother is constantly engaged in a whirlwind of activities, managing the myriad tasks that keep a household running smoothly while simultaneously nurturing her family's physical, emotional, and social well-being.

One of the remarkable qualities of a housewife mother is her ability to multitask effectively. Throughout the day, she seamlessly transitions between various roles and responsibilities, whether it's preparing meals, doing laundry, cleaning the house, or managing finances. With remarkable efficiency and resourcefulness, she tackles each task with determination and grace, ensuring that her family's needs are met with love and care.

Despite the demands of managing a household, a housewife mother also plays a pivotal role in fostering the intellectual and creative development of her children. Through engaging activities, stimulating conversations, and a nurturing environment, she creates a space where her children can explore their interests, pursue their passions, and unlock their potential. Whether it's helping with homework, encouraging extracurricular activities, or instilling values of perseverance and resilience, she serves as a constant source of support and guidance in her children's journey towards excellence.

In addition to her role as a caregiver and educator, a housewife mother also fulfills the vital role of a supportive partner and confidante to her husband. She provides emotional support, companionship, and a safe haven in times of joy and sorrow, standing by her husband's side through life's ups and downs. With unwavering love and devotion, she nurtures the bonds of marriage, fostering a relationship built on mutual respect, trust, and understanding.

Furthermore, a housewife mother often extends her care and compassion beyond the confines of her immediate family to include her in-laws and parents. Whether it's offering a listening ear, providing practical assistance, or simply being a source of comfort and encouragement, she embodies the spirit of selflessness and generosity, enriching the lives of those around her with her boundless love and kindness.

In essence, the remarkable ability of a housewife mother to balance multiple roles and responsibilities while nurturing her family's well-being is a testament to her strength, resilience, and unwavering dedication. Through her tireless efforts and sacrificial love, she creates an environment where genius talents can thrive, children can flourish, and relationships can blossom. Indeed, the contributions of a housewife mother are immeasurable, shaping the lives of her loved ones and leaving a lasting legacy of love, compassion, and resilience for generations to come.

Consider the stories of the world's most renowned figures—the visionaries, the innovators, the leaders—who have left an indelible imprint on history. Behind each of these towering figures stands a mother, a silent force whose influence transcends time and space. From nurturing their children's dreams to instilling values of resilience and perseverance, mothers play an indispensable role in shaping the destiny of future generations.

Take, for example, the story of Mahatma Gandhi, the revered leader of India's independence movement. Behind his towering legacy of nonviolence and civil disobedience stood his mother, Putlibai Gandhi, whose unwavering faith and moral guidance shaped his character and ideals. It was her steadfast belief in the power of truth and compassion that laid the foundation for Gandhi's transformative vision of social justice and equality.

Similarly, the saga of Mother Teresa, the epitome of compassion and selflessness, is a testament to the profound impact of maternal love. Born Agnes Gonxha Bojaxhiu, Mother Teresa's unwavering devotion to serving the poorest of the poor was inspired by her mother's compassionate spirit and deep sense of empathy. It was her mother's teachings of kindness and generosity that ignited the flame of altruism within her, leading her to dedicate her life to the service of humanity.

Across cultures and continents, the stories of legends and luminaries are intertwined with the timeless wisdom and boundless love of mothers. Whether it be the entrepreneurial spirit of Dhirubhai Ambani, the artistic genius of Rabindranath Tagore, or the scientific curiosity of Kalpana Chawla, behind every success story lies the guiding hand of a mother, whose love and sacrifices pave the way for greatness.

In the words of renowned author Washington Irving, "A mother is the truest friend we have, when trials, heavy and sudden, fall upon us; when adversity takes the place of prosperity; when friends who rejoice with us in our sunshine, desert us when troubles thicken around us, still will she cling to us, and endeavor by her kind precepts and counsels to dissipate the clouds of darkness, and cause peace to return to our hearts."

Famous Motivational & Inspirational Quotes

1. Abraham Lincoln(34 quotes)
2. Albert Einstein(53 quotes)
3. Anthony Robbins(34 quotes)
4. Brian Tracey(24 quotes)
5. Dale Carnegie(25 quotes)
6. Dennis Waitley(32 quotes)
7. Donald Trump(11 quotes)
8. Earl Nightingale(25 quotes)
9. Jim Rohn(28 quotes)
10. Mark Victor Hansen(17 quotes)
11. Napoleon Hill(37 quotes)
12. Norman Vincent Peale(50 quotes)
13. Paul Sweeney(7 quotes)
14. Ralph Waldo Emerson(38 quotes)
15. Robert H. Schuller(30 quotes)
16. Robert T. Kiyosaki(11 quotes)
17. Thomas Edison(51 quotes)
18. Thomas Jefferson(22 quotes)
19. W. Clement Stone(25 quotes)
20. Zig Ziglar(27 quotes)
21. More Famous Quotes(156 quotes)

Abraham Lincoln
34 quotes

1. My father taught me to work; he did not teach me to love it.

2. Common looking people are the best in the world: that is the reason the Lord makes so many of them.

3. How many legs does a dog have if you call the tail a leg? Four. Calling a tail a leg doesn't make it a leg.

4. And in the end it's not the years in your life that count. It's the life in your years.

5. My experience has taught me that a man who has no vices has damned few virtues.

6. Let not him who is houseless pull down the house of another, but let him work diligently and build one for himself, thus by example assuring that his own shall be safe from violence when built.

7. Will springs from the two elements of moral sense and self-interest.

8. My great concern is not whether you have failed, but whether you are content with your failure.

9. The way for a young man to rise is to improve himself in every way he can, never suspecting that anybody wishes to hinder him.

10. I am a slow walker, but I never walk backwards.

11. I will prepare and some day my chance will come.

12. I want it said of me by those who knew me best; that I always plucked a thistle and planted a flower where I thought a flower would grow.

13. I never had a policy; I have just tried to do my very best each and every day.

14. If there is anything that a man can do well, I say let him do it. Give him a chance.

15. You cannot escape the responsibility of tomorrow by evading it today.

16. Nearly all men can stand adversity, but if you want to test a man's character, give him power.

17. I do not think much of a man who is not wiser today than he was yesterday.

18. Fourscore and seven years ago our fathers brought forth on this continent, a new nation, conceived in Liberty, and dedicated to the proposition that all men are created equal.

19. People are just as happy as they make up their minds to be.

20. Nearly all men can stand adversity, but if you want to test a man's character, give him power.

21. With malice toward none, with charity for all.

22. That some should be rich, shows that others may become rich, and, hence, is just encouragement to industry and enterprise.

23. Always bear in mind, that your own resolution to succeed is more important than any other thing.

24. Determine that the thing can and shall be done, and then we shall find the way.

25. I have noticed that folks are generally about as happy as they make up their minds to be.

26. I don't think much of a man who is not wiser today than he was yesterday.

27. The best thing about the future is that it comes only one day at a time.

28. When I do good, I feel good. When I do bad, I feel bad. That's my religion.

29. You cannot escape the responsibility of tomorrow by evading it today.

30. The best thing about the future is that it comes only one day at a time.

31. I don't like the man. I must get to know him better.

32. Those who deny freedom to others, deserve it not for themselves; and under a just God, can not long retain it.

33. What ever you are be a good one.

34. Always bear in mind that your own resolution to succeed is more important than any other one thing.

Albert Einstein
53 quotes

1. Any intelligent fool can make things bigger, more complex, and more violent. It takes a touch of genius—and a lot of courage—to move in the opposite direction.

2. Imagination is more important than knowledge.

3. Gravitation is not responsible for people falling in love.

4. I want to know God's thoughts; the rest are details.

5. The hardest thing in the world to understand is the income tax.

6. Reality is merely an illusion, albeit a very persistent one.

7. The only real valuable thing is intuition.

8. A person starts to live when he can live outside himself.

9. I am convinced that He (God) does not play dice.

10. God is subtle but he is not malicious.

11. Weakness of attitude becomes weakness of character.

12. I never think of the future. It comes soon enough.

13. The eternal mystery of the world is its comprehensibility.

14. Sometimes one pays most for the things one gets for nothing.

15. Science without religion is lame. Religion without science is blind.

16. Anyone who has never made a mistake has never tried anything new.

17. Great spirits have often encountered violent opposition from weak minds.

18. Everything should be made as simple as possible, but not simpler.

19. Common sense is the collection of prejudices acquired by age eighteen.

20. Science is a wonderful thing if one does not have to earn one's living at it.

21. The secret to creativity is knowing how to hide your sources.

22. The only thing that interferes with my learning is my education.

23. God does not care about our mathematical difficulties. He integrates empirically.

24. The whole of science is nothing more than a refinement of everyday thinking.

25. Technological progress is like an axe in the hands of a pathological criminal.

26. Peace cannot be kept by force. It can only be achieved by understanding.

27. The most incomprehensible thing about the world is that it is comprehensible.

28. We can't solve problems by using the same kind of thinking we used when we created them.

29. Education is what remains after one has forgotten everything he learned in school.

30. The important thing is not to stop questioning. Curiosity has its own reason for existing.

31. Do not worry about your difficulties in Mathematics. I can assure you mine are still greater.

32. Equations are more important to me, because politics is for the present, but an equation is something for eternity.

33. If A is a success in life, then A equals x plus y plus z. Work is x; y is play; and z is keeping your mouth shut.

34. Two things are infinite: the universe and human stupidity; and I'm not sure about the the universe.

35. As far as the laws of mathematics refer to reality, they are not certain, as far as they are certain, they do not refer to reality.

36. Whoever undertakes to set himself up as a judge of Truth and Knowledge is shipwrecked by the laughter of the gods.

37. I know not with what weapons World War III will be fought, but World War IV will be fought with sticks and stones.

38. In order to form an immaculate member of a flock of sheep one must, above all, be a sheep.

39. The fear of death is the most unjustified of all fears, for there's no risk of accident for someone who's dead.

40. Too many of us look upon Americans as dollar chasers. This is a cruel libel, even if it is reiterated thoughtlessly by the Americans themselves.

41. Heroism on command, senseless violence, and all the loathsome nonsense that goes by the name of patriotism—how passionately I hate them!

42. No, this trick won't work...How on earth are you ever going to explain in terms of chemistry and physics so important a biological phenomenon as first love?

43. My religion consists of a humble admiration of the illimitable superior spirit who reveals himself in the slight details we are able to perceive with our frail and feeble mind.

44. Yes, we have to divide up our time like that, between our politics and our equations. But to me our equations are

far more important, for politics are only a matter of present concern. A mathematical equation stands forever.

45. The release of atom power has changed everything except our way of thinking...the solution to this problem lies in the heart of mankind. If only I had known, I should have become a watchmaker.

46. Great spirits have always found violent opposition from mediocrities. The latter cannot understand it when a man does not thoughtlessly submit to hereditary prejudices but honestly and courageously uses his intelligence.

47. The most beautiful thing we can experience is the mysterious. It is the source of all true art and all science. He to whom this emotion is a stranger, who can no longer pause to wonder and stand rapt in awe, is as good as dead: his eyes are closed.

48. A man's ethical behavior should be based effectually on sympathy, education, and social ties; no religious basis is necessary. Man would indeeded be in a poor way if he had to be restrained by fear of punishment and hope of reward after death.

49. The further the spiritual evolution of mankind advances, the more certain it seems to me that the path to genuine religiosity does not lie through the fear of life, and the fear of death, and blind faith, but through striving after rational knowledge.

50. Now he has departed from this strange world a little ahead of me. That means nothing. People like us, who believe in physics, know that the distinction between past, present, and future is only a stubbornly persistent illusion.

51. You see, wire telegraph is a kind of a very, very long cat. You pull his tail in New York and his head is meowing in Los Angeles. Do you understand this? And radio operates exactly the same way: you send signals here, they receive them there. The only difference is that there is no cat.

52. One had to cram all this stuff into one's mind for the examinations, whether one liked it or not. This coercion had such a deterring effect on me that, after I had passed the final examination, I found the consideration of any scientific problems distasteful to me for an entire year.

53. one of the strongest motives that lead men to art and science is escape from

everyday life with its painful crudity and hopeless dreariness, from the fetters of one's own ever-shifting desires. A finely tempered nature longs to escape from the personal life into the world of objective perception and thought.

54. He who joyfully marches to music rank and file, has already earned my contempt. He has been given a large brain by mistake, since for him the spinal cord would surely suffice. This disgrace to civilization should be done away with at once. Heroism at command, how violently I hate all this, how despicable and ignoble war is; I would rather be torn to shreds than be a part of so base an action. It is my conviction that killing under the cloak of war is nothing but an act of murder.

55. A human being is a part of a whole, called by us _universe_, a part limited in time and space. He experiences himself, his thoughts and feelings as something separated from the rest. a kind of optical delusion of his consciousness. This

delusion is a kind of prison for us, restricting us to our personal desires and to affection for a few persons nearest to us.

Our task must be to free ourselves from this prison by widening our circle of compassion to embrace all living creatures and the whole of nature in its beauty.

Anthony Robbins
48 quotes

1. A real decision is measured by the fact that you've taken a new action. If there's no action, you haven't truly decided.

2. Beliefs have the power to create and the power to destroy. Human beings have the awesome ability to take any experience of their lives and create a meaning that disempowers them or one that can literally save their lives.

3. Commit to CANI! - Constant And Never-ending Improvement

4. For changes to be of any true value, they've got to be lasting and consistent.

5. I challenge you to make your life a masterpiece. I challenge you to join the ranks of those people who live what they teach, who walk their talk.

6. I've come to believe that all my past failure and frustration were actually laying the foundation for the understandings that have created the new level of living I now enjoy.

7. If you do what you've always done, you'll get what you've always gotten.

8. In essence, if we want to direct our lives, we must take control of our consistent actions. It's not what we do once in a while that shapes our lives, but what we do consistently.

9. In life you need either inspiration or desperation.

10. It is in your moments of decision that your destiny is shaped.

11. It is not what we get. But who we become, what we contribute... that gives meaning to our lives.

12. It not knowing what to do, it's doing what you know.

13. It's not the events of our lives that shape us, but our beliefs as to what those events mean.

14. Life is a gift, and it offers us the privilege, opportunity, and responsibility to give something back by becoming more.

15. Live with passion!

16. Most people have no idea of the giant capacity we can immediately command when we focus all of our resources on mastering a single area of our lives.

17. My definition of success is to live your life in a way that causes you to feel a ton of pleasure and very little pain - and because of your lifestyle, have the people around you feel a lot more pleasure than they do pain.

18. Once you have mastered time, you will understand how true it is that most people overestimate what they can accomplish in a year - and underestimate what they can achieve in a decade!

19. One reason so few of us achieve what we truly want is that we never direct our focus; we never concentrate our power. Most people dabble their way through life, never deciding to master anything in particular.

20. Only those who have learned the power of sincere and selfless contribution experience life's deepest joy: true fulfillment.

21. Passion is the genesis of genius.

22. People are not lazy. They simply have impotent goals - that is, goals that do not inspire them.

23. Setting goals is the first step in turning the invisible into the visible.

24. Success comes from taking the initiative and following up... persisting... eloquently expressing the depth of your love.

What simple action could you take today to produce a new momentum toward success in your life?

25. Surmounting difficulty is the crucible that forms character.

26. Take control of your consistent emotions and begin to consciously and deliberately reshape your daily experience of life.

27. The higher your energy level, the more efficient your body The more efficient your body, the better you feel and the more you will use your talent to produce outstanding results.

28. The meeting of preparation with opportunity generates the offspring we call luck.

29. The path to success is to take massive, determined action.

30. The secret of success is learning how to use pain and pleasure instead of having pain and pleasure use you. If you do that, you're in control of your life. If you don't, life controls you.

31. The truth is that we can learn to condition our minds, bodies, and emotions to link pain or pleasure to whatever we choose. By changing what we link pain and pleasure to, we will instantly change our behaviors.

32. The way we communicate with others and with ourselves ultimately determines the quality of our lives.

33. There is no greatness without a passion to be great, whether it's the aspiration of an athlete or an artist, a scientist, a parent, or a businessperson.

34. There is no such thing as failure. There are only results.

35. There's always a way - if you're committed.

36. There's no abiding success without commitment.

37. To effectively communicate, we must realize that we are all different in the way we perceive the world and use this understanding as a guide to our communication with others.

38. Want to learn to eat a lot? Here it is: Eat a little. That way, you will be around long enough to eat a lot.

39. We are the only beings on the planet who lead such rich internal lives that it's not the events that matter most to us, but rather, it's how we interpret those events that will determine how we think about ourselves and how we will act in the future.

40. We aren't in an information age, we are in an entertainment age.

41. We can change our lives. We can do, have, and be exactly what we wish.

42. We will act consistently with our view of who we truly are, whether that view is accurate or not.

43. What we can or cannot do, what we consider possible or impossible, is rarely a function of our true capability. It is more likely a function of our beliefs about who we are.

44. Whatever happens, take responsibility!

45. When people are like each other they tend to like each other.

46. You always succeed in producing a result.

47. You see, in life, lots of people know what to do, but few people actually do what they know. Knowing is not enough! You must take action.

48. You see, it's never the environment; it's never the events of our lives, but the meaning we attach to the events - how we interpret them - that shapes who we are today and who we'll become tomorrow.

Brian Tracey
24 quotes

1. The more credit you give away, the more will come back to you. The more you help others, the more they will want to help you.

2. Successful people are always looking for opportunities to help others. Unsuccessful people are always asking, "What's in it for me?

3. Your decision to be, have and do something out of ordinary entails facing difficulties that are out of the ordinary as well. Sometimes your greatest asset is simply your ability to stay with it longer than anyone else.

4. Those people who develop the ability to continuously acquire new and better forms of knowledge that they can apply to their work and to their lives will be the movers and shakers in our society for the indefinite future.

5. No one lives long enough to learn everything they need to learn starting from scratch. To be successful, we absolutely, positively have to find people who have already paid the price to learn the things that we need to learn to achieve our goals.

6. It doesn't matter where you are coming from. All that matters is where you are going.

7. If you raise your children to feel that they can accomplish any goal or task they decide upon, you will have succeeded as a parent and you will have given your children the greatest of all blessings.

8. Develop an attitude of gratitude, and give thanks for everything that happens to you, knowing that every step forward is a step toward achieving something bigger and better than your current situation.

9. All successful people men and women are big dreamers. They imagine what their future could be, ideal in every respect, and then they work every day toward their distant vision, that goal or purpose.

10. You cannot control what happens to you, but you can control your attitude toward what happens to you, and in that, you will be mastering change rather than allowing it to master you.

11. I've found that luck is quite predictable. If you want more luck, take more chances. Be more active. Show up more often."

12. In life you can never be too kind or too fair; everyone you meet is carrying a heavy load. When you go through your day expressing kindness and courtesy to all you meet, you leave behind a feeling of warmth and good cheer, and you help alleviate the burdens everyone is struggling with.

13. The more you seek security, the less of it you have. But the more you seek opportunity, the more likely it is that you will achieve the security that you desire.

14. The glue that holds all relationships together—including the relationship between the leader and the led is trust, and trust is based on integrity.

15. Relationships are the hallmark of the mature person.

16. Only by contending with challenges that seem to be beyond your strength to handle at the moment you can grow more surely toward the stars.

17. Never say anything about yourself you do not want to come true.

18. The person we believe ourselves to be will always act in a manner consistent with our self-image.

19. Teamwork is so important that it is virtually impossible for you to reach the heights of your capabilities or make the money that you want without becoming very good at it.

20. We feel good about ourselves to the exact degree we feel in control of our lives.

21. The potential of the average person is like a huge ocean unsailed, a new continent unexplored, a world of possibilities waiting to be released and channeled toward some great good.

22. You have available to you, right now, a powerful supercomputer. This powerful tool has been used through-out history to take people from rags to riches, from poverty and obscurity to success and fame, from unhappiness and frustration to joy and self-fulfillment, and it can do the same for you.

23. You have within you right now, everything you need to deal with whatever the world can throw at you.

24. Success is predictable.

Dale Carnegie
25 quotes

1. If you can't sleep, then get up and do something instead of lying there and worrying. It's the worry that gets you, not the loss of sleep.

2. Are you bored with life? Then throw yourself into some work you believe in with all your heart, live for it, die for it, and you will find happiness that you had thought could never be yours.

3. If you want to win friends, make it a point to remember them. If you remember my name, you pay me a subtle compliment; you indicate that I have made an impression on you. Remember my name and you add to my feeling of importance.

4. Take a chance! All life is a chance. The man who goes the furthest is generally the one who is willing to do and dare.

5. Don't be afraid to give your best to what seemingly are small jobs. Every time you conquer one it makes you that much stronger. If you do the little jobs well, the big ones tend to take care of themselves.

6. If you believe in what you are doing, then let nothing hold you up in your work. Much of the best work of the world has been done against seeming impossibilities. The thing is to get the work done.

7. It isn't what you have, or who you are, or where you are, or what you are doing that makes you happy or unhappy. It is what you think about.

8. The ideas I stand for are not mine. I borrowed them from Socrates. I swiped them from Chesterfield. I stole them from

Jesus. And I put them in a book. If you don't like their rules whose would you use?

9. One of the most tragic things I know about human nature is that all of us tend to put off living. We are all dreaming of some magical rose garden over the horizon- instead of enjoying the roses blooming outside our windows today."

10. Any fool can criticize, condemn, and complain—and most fools do.

11. Most of the important things in the world have been accomplished by people who have kept on trying when there seemed to be no help at all.

12. You can make more friends in two months by becoming interested in other people than you can in two years by trying to get other people interested in you.

13. Remember happiness doesn't depend on who you are or what you have; it depends solely upon what you think.

14. The man who goes farthest is generally the one who is willing to do and dare. The sure-thing boat never gets far from shore."

15. Success is getting what you want. Happiness is wanting what you get.

16. Those convinced against their will are of the same opinion still.

17. I deal with the obvious. I present, reiterate and glorify the obvious—because the obvious is what people need to be told.

18. The royal road to a man's heart is to talk to him about the things he treasures most.

19. There are four ways, and only four ways, in which we have contact with the world. We are evaluated and classified by

these four contacts: what we do, how we look, what we say, and how we say it.

20. Your purpose is to make your audience see what you saw, hear what you heard, feel what you felt. Relevant detail, couched in concrete, colorful language, is the best way to recreate the incident as it happened and to picture it for the audience.

21. Flaming enthusiasm, backed up by horse sense and persistence, is the quality that most frequently makes for success.

22. If you want to be enthusiastic, act enthusiastic.

23. There is only one way... to get anybody to do anything. And that is by making the other person want to do it.

24. When fate hands us a lemon, let's try to make a lemonade.

25. The successful man will profit from his mistakes and try again in a different way.

Dennis Waitley
32 quotes

1. Mistakes are painful when they happen, but years later a collection of mistakes is what is called experience.

2. If you believe you can, you probably can. If you believe you won't, you most assuredly won't. Belief is the ignition switch that gets you off the launching pad.

3. Forget about the consequences of failure. Failure is only a temporary change in direction to set you straight for your next success.

4. As long as we are persistence in our pursuit of our deepest destiny, we will continue to grow. We cannot choose the day or time when we will fully bloom. It happens in its own time.

5. Don't dwell on what went wrong. Instead, focus on what to do next. Spend your energies on moving forward toward finding the answer.

6. Expect the best, plan for the worst, and prepare to be surprised.

7. You must learn from your past mistakes, but not lean on your past successes.

8. Our limitations and success will be based, most often, on your own expectations for ourselves. What the mind dwells upon, the body acts upon.

9. The reason most people never reach their goals is that they don't define them, learn about them, or even seriously consider them as believable or achievable. Winners can tell you where they are going, what they plan to do along the way, and who will be sharing the adventure with them.

10. To establish true self-esteem we must concentrate on our successes and forget about the failures and the negatives in our lives.

11. Failure should be our teacher, not our undertaker. Failure is delay, not defeat. It is a temporary detour, not a dead end. Failure is something we can avoid only by saying nothing, doing nothing, and being nothing.

12. It's not what you are that holds you back, it's what you think you are not.

13. Where there is life, there is hope. Where there are hopes, there are dreams. Where there are vivid dreams repeated, they become goals. Goals become the action plans and game plans that winners dwell on in intricate detail, knowing that achievement is almost automatic when the goal becomes an inner commitment. The response to the challenges of life—purpose—is the healing balm that enables each of us to face up to adversity and strife.

14. When you make a mistake or get ridiculed or rejected, look at mistakes as learning experiences, and ridicule as ignorance. Look at rejection as part of one performance, not as a turn down of the performer.

15. Luck happens when opportunity encounters the prepared mind.

16. You must consider the bottom line, but make it integrity before profits.

17. Losers make promises they often break. Winners make commitments they always keep.

18. A life lived with integrity—even if it lacks the trappings of fame and fortune is a shinning star in whose light others may follow in the years to come.

19. No man or woman is an island. To exist just for yourself is meaningless. You can achieve the most satisfaction when you feel related to some greater purpose in life, something greater than yourself.

20. Procrastination is the fear of success. People procrastinate because they are afraid of the success that they know will result if they move ahead now. Because success is heavy, carries a responsibility with it, it is much easier to procrastinate and live on the 'someday I'll' philosophy.

21. Get excited and enthusiastic about you own dream. This excitement is like a forest fire—you can smell it, taste it, and see it from a mile away.

22. Life is not accountable to us. We are accountable to life.

23. We have got to have a dream if we are going to make a dream come true.

24. Out of need springs desire, and out of desire springs the energy and the will to win.

25. Life is a do-it yourself project.

26. Life is the movie you see through your own eyes. It makes little difference what's happening out there. It's how you take it that counts.

27. Winners take time to relish their work, knowing that scaling the mountain is what makes the view from the top so exhilarating.

28. Happiness cannot be traveled to, owned, earned, worn or consumed. Happiness is the spiritual experience of living every minute with love, grace and gratitude.

29. The greatest gifts you can give your children are the roots of responsibility and the wings of independence.

30. Love is a daily, mutual exchange of value.

31. A smile is the light in your window that tells others that there is a caring, sharing person inside.

32. Time is an equal opportunity employer. Each human being has exactly the same number of hours and minutes every day. Rich people can't buy more hours. Scientists can't invent new minutes. And you can't save time to spend it on another day. Even so, time is amazingly fair and forgiving. No matter how much time you've wasted in the past, you still have an entire tomorrow.

Donald Trump
11 quotes

1. I try to learn from the past, but I plan for the future by focusing exclusively on the present. That's were the fun is.

2. The point is that you can't be too greedy.

3. A little more moderation would be good. Of course, my life hasn't exactly been one of moderation.

4. Sometimes by losing a battle you find a new way to win the war.

5. I try to learn from the past, but I plan for the future by focusing exclusively on the present. That's were the fun is. -Donald Trump.

6. Part of being a winner is knowing when enough is enough. Sometimes you have to give up the fight and walk away, and move on to something that's more productive.

7. I'm a bit of a P. T. Barnum. I make stars out of everyone.

8. Experience taught me a few things. One is to listen to your gut, no matter how good something sounds on paper. The second is that you're generally better off sticking with what you know. And the third is that sometimes your best investments are the ones you don't make.

9. You have to think anyway, so why not think big?

10. Deals are my art form. Other people paint beautifully on canvas or write wonderful poetry. I like making deals, preferably big deals. That's how I get my kicks.

11. Money was never a big motivation for me, except as a way to keep score. The real excitement is playing the game.

Earl Nightingale
25 quotes

1. You become what you think about.

2. Our attitude toward life determines life's attitude towards us.

3. People with goals succeed because they know where they're going.

4. Success is the progressive realization of a worthy goal or ideal

5. Open your ears before you open your mouth, it may surprise your eyes!

6. Am I motivated by what I really want out of life — or am I mass-motivated?

7. Your world is a living expression of how you are using and have used your mind

8. We can let circumstances rule us, or we can take charge and rule our lives from within

9. All you need is the plan, the road map, and the courage to press on to your destination

10. We can help others in the world more by making the most of yourself than in any other way.

11. Whenever we're afraid, its because we don't know enough. If we understood enough, we would never be afraid.

12. Whatever we plant in our subconscious mind and nourish with repetition and emotion will one day become a reality

13. People are where they are because that's exactly where they really want to be ... whether they'll admit that or not

14. Wherever there is danger, there lurks opportunity; whenever there is opportunity, there lurks danger. The two are inseparable. They go together.

15. A great attitude does much more than turn on the lights in our worlds; it seems to magically connect us to all sorts of serendipitous opportunities that were somehow absent before the change.

16. Spoken about Earl Nightingale by Steve King, radio announcer and good friend: Earl Nightingale never let a day go by that he didn't learn something new and, in turn pass it on to others. It was his consuming passion.

17. We are at our very best, and we are happiest, when we are fully engaged in work we enjoy on the journey toward the goal we've established for ourselves. It gives meaning to our time off and comfort to our sleep. It makes everything else in life so wonderful, so worthwhile.

18. For a person to build a rich and rewarding life for himself there are certain qualities and bits of knowledge that he needs to acquire. There are also things, harmful attitudes, superstitions, and emotions that he needs to chip away. A person needs to chip away everything that doesn't look like the person he or she most wants to become.

19. We tend to live up to our expectations.

20. You'll find boredom where there is an absence of a good idea.

21. Creativity is a natural extension of our enthusiasm.

22. Everything in the world we want to do or get done, we must do with and through people.

23. Get into a line that you will find to be a deep personal interest, something you really enjoy spending twelve to fifteen hours a day working at, and the rest of the time thinking about.

24. Learn to enjoy every minute of your life. Be happy now. Don't wait for something outside of yourself to make you happy in the future. Think how really precious is the time you have to spend, whether it's at work or with your family. Every minute should be enjoyed and savored.

25. Our first journey is to find that special place for us.

Jim Rohn
28 quotes

1. It doesn't matter which side of the fence you get off on sometimes. What matters most is getting off. You cannot make progress without making decisions.

2. Whoever renders service to many puts himself in line for greatness—great wealth, great return, great satisfaction, great reputation, and great joy.

3. For every disciplined effort there is a multiple reward.

4. Formal education will make you a living; self-education will make you a fortune.

5. Give whatever you are doing and whoever you are with the gift of your attention.

6. Words do two major things: They provide food for the mind and create light for understanding and awareness.

7. The worst thing one can do is not to try, to be aware of what one wants and not give in to it, to spend years in silent hurt wondering if something could have materialized—never knowing.

8. The major reason for setting a goal is for what it makes of you to accomplish it. What it makes of you will always be the far greater value than what you get.

9. To solve any problem, here are three questions to ask yourself: First, what could I do? Second, what could I read? And third, who could I ask?

10. Formal education will make you a living, self education will make you a fortune.

11. Discipline is the bridge between goals and accomplishment.

12. The book you don't read cant help.

13. Success is neither magical or mysterious. Success is the natural consequence of consistently applying the basic fundamentals.

14. Success is nothing more than a few simple disciplines, practiced every day...

15. Success is not to be pursued; it is to be attracted by the person you become.

16. Either you run the day or the day runs you.

17. Whatever good things we build end up building us.

18. We must all suffer one of two things: the pain of discipline or the pain of regret or disappointment.

19. Take advantage of every opportunity to practice your communication skills so that when important occasions arise, you will have the gift, the style, the sharpness, the clarity, and the emotions to affect other people.

20. Effective communication is 20% what you know and 80% how you feel about what you know.

21. Some people plant in the spring and leave in the summer. If you're signed up for a season, see it through. You don't have to stay forever, but at least stay until you see it through.

22. Take care of your body. It's the only place you have to live.

23. Don't wish it were easier, wish you were better.

24. You must take personal responsibility. You cannot change the circumstances, the seasons, or the wind, but you can change yourself. That is something you have charge of.

25. Don't say, "If I could, I would." Say, "If I can, I will"

26. Every life form seems to strive to its maximum except human beings. How tall will a tree grow? As tall as it possibly

can. Human beings, on the other hand, have been given the dignity of choice. You can choose to be all or you can choose to be less. Why not stretch up to the full measure of the challenge and see what all you can do?

27. Indecision is the thief of opportunity.

28. You cannot change your destination overnight, but you can change your direction overnight.

Mark Victor Hansen
18 quotes

1. Ideas attract money, time, talents, skills, energy and other complementary ideas that will bring them into reality.

2. Dedicate yourself to the good you deserve and desire for yourself. Give yourself peace of mind. You deserve to be happy. You deserve delight.

3. I never let my subject get in the way of what I want to talk about.

4. I want to talk with people who care about things that matter that will make a life- changing difference

5. You control your future, your destiny. What you think about comes about. By recording your dreams and goals on paper, you set in motion the process of becoming the person you most want to be. Put your future in good hands—your own.

6. Don't wait until everything is just right. It will never be perfect. There will always be challenges, obstacles and less than perfect conditions. So what. Get started now. With each step you take, you will grow stronger and stronger, more and more skilled, more and more self-confident and more and more successful.

7. Don't think it, ink it.

8. In imagination, there's no limitation.

9. When your self-worth goes up, your net worth goes up with it.

10. True or true? Yes or yes?.

11. Imitate until you emulate; match and surpass those who launched you. It's the highest form of thankfulness.

12. Now is the only time there is. Make your now wow, your minutes miracles, and your days pay. Your life will have been magnificently lived and invested, and when you die you will have made a difference.

13. End your day by privately looking directly into your eyes in the mirror and saying, 'I love you!' Do this for thirty days and watch how you transform.

14. Your belief determines your action and your action determines your results, but first you have to believe.

15. The more goals you set - the more goals you get.

16. Predetermine the objectives you want to accomplish. Think big, act big and set out to accomplish big results.

17. With vision, every person, organization and country can flourish. The Bible says, 'Without vision we perish.

18. Whatever you need more of is what you need to tithe some.

Napoleon Hill
37 quotes

1. The best job goes to the person who can get it done without passing the buck or coming back with excuses.

2. Do not wait; the time will never be "just right." Start where you stand, and work with whatever tools you may have at your command, and better tools will be found as you go along.

3. It is always your next move.

4. No one can make you jealous, angry, vengeful, or greedy—unless you let him.

5. The battle is all over except the "shouting" when one knows what is wanted and has made up his mind to get it, whatever the price may be.

6. The starting point of all achievement is desire. Keep this constantly in mind. Weak desires bring weak results, just as a small amount of fire makes a small amount of heat.

7. Everyone enjoys doing the kind of work for which he is best suited.

8. It has always been my belief that a man should do his best, regardless of how much he receives for his services, or the number of people he may be serving or the class of people served.

9. When defeat comes, accept it as a signal that your plans are not sound, rebuild those plans, and set sail once more toward your coveted goal.

10. The most common cause of fear of old age is associated with the possibility of poverty.

11. There is one quality which one must possess to win, and that is definiteness of purpose, the knowledge of what one wants, and a burning desire to possess it.

12. Ideas... they have the power...

13. First comes thought; then organization of that thought, into ideas and plans; then transformation of those plans into reality. The beginning, as you will observe, is in your imagination.

14. There is always room for those who can be relied upon to delivery the goods when they say they will.

15. Just as our eyes need light in order to see, our minds need ideas in order to conceive.

16. Money without brains is always dangerous.

17. War grows out of the desire of the individual to gain advantage at the expense of his fellow men.

18. Persistence is to the character of man as carbon is to steel.

19. Reduce your plan to writing. The moment you complete this, you will have definitely given concrete form to the intangible desire.

20. Don't wait. The time will never be just right.

21. Think and grow rich.

22. Every person who wins in any undertaking must be willing to cut all sources of retreat. Only by doing so can one be sure of maintaining that state of mind known as a burning desire to win—essential to success.

23. The ladder of success is never crowded at the top.

24. All great truths are simple in final analysis, and easily understood; if they are not, they are not great truths.

25. If you cannot do great things, do small things in a great way.

26. No man can succeed in a line of endeavor which he does not like.

27. What we do not see, what most of us never suspect of existing, is the silent but irresistible power which comes to the rescue of those who fight on in the face of discouragement.

28. The majority of men meet with failure because of their lack of persistence in creating new plans to take the place of those which fail.

29. The most interesting thing about a postage stamp is the persistence with which it sticks to its job.

30. There is always room for those who can be relied upon to delivery the goods when they say they will.

31. Strength and growth come only through continuous effort and struggle...

32. It is literally true that you can succeed best and quickest by helping others to succeed.

33. No alibi will save you from accepting the responsibility.

34. You might well remember that nothing can bring you success but yourself.

35. Indecision is the seedling of fear.

36. Procrastination is the bad habit of putting of until the day after tomorrow what should have been done the day before yesterday.

37. Big pay and little responsibility are circumstances seldom found together.

Norman Vincent Peale
50 quotes

1. Empty pockets never held anyone back. Only empty heads and empty hearts can do that.

2. Live your life and forget your age.

3. First thing every morning before you arise say out loud, "I believe," three times.

4. When you become detached mentally from yourself and concentrate on helping other people with their difficulties, you will be able to cope with your own more effectively. Somehow, the act of self-giving is a personal power-releasing factor.

5. There is a real magic in enthusiasm. It spells the difference between mediocrity and accomplishment.

6. One of the greatest moments in anybody's developing experience is when he no longer tries to hide from himself but determines to get acquainted with himself as he really is.

7. Stand up to your obstacles and do something about them. You will find that they haven't half the strength you think they have.

8. Become a possibilitarian. No matter how dark things seem to be or actually are, raise your sights and see possibilities—always see them, for they're always there.

9. Every problem has in it the seeds of its own solution. If you don't have any problems, you don't get any seeds.

10. It is of practical value to learn to like yourself. Since you must spend so much time with yourself you might as well get some satisfaction out of the relationship.

11. We struggle with the complexities and avoid the simplicities.

12. The "how" thinker gets problems solved effectively because he wastes no time with futile "ifs."

13. People become really quite remarkable when they start thinking that they can do things. When they believe in themselves they have the first secret of success.

14. Never talk defeat. Use words like hope, belief, faith, victory.

15. Joy increases as you give it, and diminishes as you try to keep it for yourself. In giving it, you will accumulate a deposit of joy greater than you ever believed possible.

16. Those who are fired with an enthusiastic idea and who allow it to take hold and dominate their thoughts find that new worlds open for them. As long as enthusiasm holds out, so will new opportunities.

17. Practice hope. As hopefulness becomes a habit, you can achieve a permanently happy spirit.

18. If you want to get somewhere you have to know where you want to go and how to get there. Then never, never, never give up.

19. Drop the idea that you are Atlas carrying the world on your shoulders. The world would go on even without you. Don't take yourself so seriously.

20. In every difficult situation is potential value. Believe this, then begin looking for it.

21. The more you lose yourself in something bigger than yourself, the more energy you will have.

22. The "how" thinker gets problems solved effectively because he wastes no time with futile "ifs" but goes right to work on the creative "how."

23. Resentment or grudges do no harm to the person against whom you hold these feelings but every day and every night of your life, they are eating at you.

24. When a problem comes along, study it until you are completely knowledgeable. Then find that weak spot, break the problem apart, and the rest will be easy.

25. Understanding can overcome any situation, however mysterious or insurmountable it may appear to be.

26. The mind, ever the willing servant, will respond to boldness, for boldness, in effect, is a command to deliver mental resources.

27. Enthusiasm releases the drive to carry you over obstacles and adds significance to all you do.

28. It's always too soon to quit!

29. Cushion the painful effects of hard blows by keeping the enthusiasm going strong, even if doing so requires struggle.

30. Our happiness depends on the habit of mind we cultivate. So practice happy thinking every day. Cultivate the merry heart, develop the happiness habit, and life will become a continual feast.

31. Life's blows cannot break a person whose spirit is warmed at the fire of enthusiasm.

32. You can be greater than anything that can happen to you.

33. One way to become enthusiastic is to look for the plus sign. To make progress in any difficult situation, you have to start with what's right about it and build on that.

34. When you wholeheartedly adopt a 'with all your heart' attitude and go all out with the positive principle, you can do incredible things.

35. Watch your manner of speech if you wish to develop a peaceful state of mind. Start each day by affirming peaceful, contented and happy attitudes and your days will tend to be pleasant and successful.

36. To go fast, row slowly.

37. Anybody can do just about anything with himself that he really wants to and makes up his mind to do. We are all capable of greater things than we realize.

38. Go forward confidently, energetically attacking problems, expecting favorable outcomes.

39. Yesterday ended last night. Every day is a new beginning. Learn the skill of forgetting. And move on.

40. Believe it is possible to solve your problem. Tremendous things happen to the believer. So believe the answer will come. It will.

41. The way to happiness: keep your heart free from hate, your mind from worry. Live simply, expect little, give much. Fill your life with love. Scatter sunshine. Forget self, think of others. Do as you would be done by. Try this for a week and you will be surprised.

42. The positive thinker is a hard-headed, tough-minded, and factual realist. He sees all the difficulties clearly... which is more than can be said for the average negative thinker. But he sees more than difficulties—he tries to see the solutions of those difficulties.

43. Practice loving people. It is true that this requires effort and continued practice, for some are not very lovable, or so it seems - with emphasis on "seems." Every person has lovable qualities when you really learn to know him.

44. Never react emotionally to criticism. Analyze yourself to determine whether it is justified. If it is, correct yourself. Otherwise, go on about your business.

45. When you are afraid, do the thing you are afraid of and soon you will lose your fear of it.

46. The more you venture to live greatly, the more you will find within you what it takes to get on top of things and stay there.

47. If you want things to be different, perhaps the answer is to become different yourself.

48. Remember, there is no situation so completely hopeless that something constructive cannot be done about it. When faced with a minus, ask yourself what you can do to make it a plus. A person practicing this attitude will extract undreamed-of outcomes from the most unpromising situations. Realize that there are no hopeless situations; there are only people who take hopeless attitudes.

49. Believe that you are bigger than your difficulties, for you are, indeed.

50. No matter how dark things seem to be or actually are, raise your sights and see the possibilities—they're always there.

Paul Sweeney
7 quotes

1. You know when you've read a good book when you turn the last page and feel a little as if you have lost a friend.

2. True success is overcoming the fear of being unsuccessful.

3. A wedding anniversary is the celebration of love, trust, partnership, tolerance, and tenacity. The order varies for any given year.

4. True success is overcoming the fear of being unsuccessful.

5. How can a society that exists on instant mashed potatoes, packaged cake mixes, frozen dinners, and instant cameras teach patience to its young?

6. How often we fail to realize our good fortune in living in a country where happiness is more than a lack of tragedy.

7. Self delusion is pulling in your stomach when you step on the scales.

Ralph Waldo Emerson
38 quotes

1. A hero is no braver than an ordinary man, but he is braver five minutes longer.

2. Beware when the great God lets loose a thinker on this planet.

3. Character is higher than intellect... A great soul will be strong to live, as well as to think.

4. Children are all foreigners.

5. Conversation is an art in which a man has all mankind for his competitors, for it is that which all are practicing every day while they live.

6. Do not be too timid and squeamish about your actions. All life is an experiment.

7. Do not go where the path may lead, go instead where there is no path and leave a trail.

8. Don't be too timid and squeamish about your actions. All life is an experiment. The more experiments you make the better.

9. Don't waste yourself in rejection, nor bark against the bad, but chant the beauty of the good.

10. Every hero becomes a bore at last.

11. Finish each day and be done with it. You have done what you could. Some blunders and absurdities no doubt crept in; forget them as soon as you can. Tomorrow is a new day; begin it well and serenely and with too high a spirit to be cumbered with your old nonsense.

12. Give all to love; obey thy heart.

13. I awoke this morning with devout thanksgiving for my friends, the old and the new.

14. I pack my trunk, embrace my friends, embark on the sea, and at last wake up in Naples, and there beside me is the Stern Fact, the Sad Self, unrelenting, identical, that I fled from.

15. If I have lost confidence in myself, I have the universe against me.

16. Insist on yourself; never imitate... Every great man is unique.

17. Let not a man guard his dignity, but let his dignity guard him.

18. Live in the sunshine, swim the sea, drink the wild air...

19. Make the most of yourself, for that is all there is of you.

20. Nature magically suits a man to his fortunes, by making them the fruit of his character.

21. Nothing can bring you peace but yourself.

22. Nothing is at last sacred but the integrity of your own mind.

23. People seem not to see that their opinion of the world is also a confession of their character.

24. Speak what you think today in words as hard as cannon-balls and tomorrow speak what tomorrow thinks in hard words again, though it contradict every thing you said today.

25. The ancestor of every action is a thought.

26. The only way to have a friend is to be one.

27. The ornament of a house is the friends who frequent it.

28. The world belongs to the energetic.

29. We do what we must, and call it by the best names.

30. Whoever is open, loyal, true; of humane and affable demeanour; honourable himself, and in his judgement of others; faithful to his word as to law, and faithful alike to God and man. such a man is a true gentleman.

31. Nothing astonishes men so much as common sense and plain dealing.

32. He who is in love is wise and is becoming wiser, sees newly every time he looks at the object beloved, drawing from it with his eyes and his mind those virtues which it possesses.

33. Trust men and they will be true to you; treat them greatly, and they will show themselves great.

34. The best effect of fine persons is felt after we have left their presence.

35. Every artist was first an amateur.

36. None of us will every accomplish anything excellent or commanding except when he listens to this whisper which is heard by him alone.

37. A man builds a fine house; and now he has a master, and a task for life; he is to furnish, watch, show it, and keep it in repair, the rest of his days.

38. The reward of a thing well done is to have done it.

Robert H. Schuller
30 quotes

1. Commit yourself to a dream nobody who tries to do something great but fails is a total failure. Why? Because he can always rest assured that he succeeded in life's most important battle—he defeated the fear of trying.

2. Yes, you can be a dreamer and a doer too, if you will remove one word from your vocabulary: impossible.

3. You can often measure a person by the size of his dream.

4. Build a dream and the dream will build you.

5. Always look at what you have left. Never look at what you have lost.

6. Commit yourself to a dream... Nobody who tries to do something great but fails is a total failure. Why? Because he can always rest assured that he succeeded in life's most important battle—he defeated the fear of trying.

7. If you listen to your fears, you will die never knowing what a great person you might have been.

8. Impossible situations can become possible miracles.

9. It takes but one positive thought when given a chance to survive and thrive to overpower an entire army of negative thoughts.

10. Let your imagination release your imprisoned possibilities.

11. Every achiever I have ever met says, "My life turned around when I began to believe in me.

12. Anyone can count the seeds in an apple, but only God can count the number of apples in a seed.

13. Most people who succeed n the face of seemingly impossible conditions are people who simply don't know how to quit.

14. Life is but a moment, death also is but another.

15. Better to do something imperfectly than to do nothing flawlessly.

16. Again and again, the impossible problem is solved when we see that the problem is only a tough decision waiting to be made.

17. What great thing would you attempt if you knew you could not fail?

18. The only place where your dream becomes impossible is in your own thinking.

19. Never cut a tree down in the wintertime. Never make a negative decision in the low time.

20. What would you attempt to do if you knew you could not fail?

21. Failure doesn't mean you are a failure... it just means you haven't succeeded yet.

22. Goals are not only absolutely necessary to motivate us. They are essential to really keep us alive.

23. Inch by inch, it's a cinch.

24. When you can't solve the problem, manage it.

25. Never bring the problem solving stage into the decision making stage. Otherwise, you surrender yourself to the problem rather than the solution.

26. Problems are not stop signs, they are guidelines.

27. Doomed are the hotheads! Unhappy are they who lose their cool and are too proud to say, "I'm sorry."

28. Let your hopes, not your hurts, shape your future.

29. Possibilitizing is overcoming while you're undergoing.

30. Always look at what you have left. Never look at what you have lost.

Robert T. Kiyosaki
11 quotes

1. Failure defeats losers, failure inspires winners.

2. Your most expensive advice is the free advice you receive from your financially struggling friends and relatives.

3. Average investors are on the outside trying to look into the inside of the company or property they are investing in.

4. It's the investor who is risky, not the investment.

5. The idea of working all your life, saving, and putting money into a retirement account is a very slow plan.

6. If you don't first handle fear and desire, and you get rich, you'll be a high pay slave.

7. To gain more abundance a person needs more skills and needs to be more creative and cooperative.

8. The unique ability to take decisive action while maintaining focus on the ultimate mission is what defines a true leader.

9. Instead of labeling and discriminating against one or the other, we need to learn to blend our gifts and complement our geniuses.

10. By asking the question "How can I afford it?" your brain is put to work.

11. One of the main reasons people are not rich is that they worry too much about things that might never happen.

Thomas Edison
51 quotes

1. Genius is one per cent inspiration and ninety-nine per cent perspiration. Accordingly, a 'genius' is often merely a talented person who has done all of his or her homework.

2. Opportunity is missed by most people because it is dressed in overalls and looks like work.

3. The first requisite for success is to develop the ability to focus and apply your mental and physical energies to the problem at hand - without growing weary. Because such thinking is often difficult, there seems to be no limit to which some people will go to avoid the effort and labor that is associated with it....

4. I never did anything worth doing entirely by accident. Almost none of my inventions came about totally by accident. They were achieved by having trained myself to endure and tolerate hard work.

5. Personally, I enjoy working about 18 hours a day. Besides the short catnaps I take each day, I average about four to five hours of sleep per night.

6. My main purpose in life is to make money so I can afford to go on creating more inventions....

7. My principal business is giving commercial value to the brilliant - but misdirected- ideas of others....

8. I am quite correctly described as 'more of a sponge than an inventor. '

9. Because I readily absorb ideas from every source - frequently starting where the last person left off - I never pick up an item without thinking of how I might improve it.

10. I am not overly impressed by the great names and reputations of those who might be trying to beat me to an invention. Its their 'ideas' that appeal to me.

11. Because ideas have to be original only with regard to their adaptation to the problem at hand, I am always extremely interested in how others have used used them....

12. A good idea is never lost. Even though its originator or possessor may die, it will someday be reborn in the mind of another....

13. I never perfected an invention that I did not think about in terms of the service it might give others... I find out what the world needs, then I proceed to invent....

14. The dove is my emblem I want to save and advance human life, not destroy it.... I am proud of the fact that I never invented weapons to kill....

15. Most of the exercise I get is from standing and walking around laboratory tables all day. I derive more benefit and entertainment from this than some of my friends and competitors get from playing games like golf.

16. If we all did the things we are really capable of doing, we would literally astound ourselves....

17. Our schools and are not teaching students to think. It is astonishing how many young people have difficulty in putting their brains definitely and systematically to work....

18. The three things that are most essential to achievement are common sense, hard work and stick-to-it-iv-ness.....

19. I have far more respect for the person with a single idea who gets there than for the person with a thousand ideas who does nothing....

20. Many of life's failures are experienced by people who did not realize how close they were to success when they gave up.

21. Pretty much everything will come to him who hustles while he waits. I believe that restlessness is discontent, and discontent is merely the first necessity of progress. Show me a thoroughly satisfied man and I will show you a failure.

22. Unfortunately, there seems to be far more opportunity out there than ability.... We should remember that good fortune often happens when opportunity meets with preparation.

23. Sometimes, all you need to invent something is a good imagination and a pile of junk....

24. Just because something doesn't do what you planned it to do in the first place doesn't mean it's useless....

25. Results? Why, man, I have gotten lots of results! If I find 10,000 ways something won't work, I haven't failed. I am not discouraged, because every wrong attempt discarded is often a step forward....

26. Surprises and reverses can serve as an incentive for great accomplishment. There are no rules here, we're just trying to accomplish something.

27. As a cure for worrying, work is far better than whiskey. I always found that, if I began to worry, the best thing I could do was focus upon doing something useful and then work very hard at it. Soon, I would forget what was troubling me.

28. Barring serious accidents, if you are not preoccupied with worry and you work hard, you can look forward to a reasonably lengthy existence. Its not the hard

work that kills, its the worrying that kills.

29. The only time I really become discouraged is when I think of all the things I would like to do and the little time I have in which to do them.

30. The thing I lose patience with the most is the clock. Its hands move too fast.

31. Time is really the only capital that any human being has and the thing that he can least afford to waste or lose...

32. From his neck down a man is worth a couple of dollars a day, from his neck up he is worth anything that his brain can produce.

33. The doctor of the future will give no medicine, but will interest his patients in the care of the human body, in diet, and in the cause and prevention of disease.

34. Whatever the mind of man creates, should be controlled by man's character.

35. Even though I am nearly deaf, I seem to be gifted with a kind of inner hearing which enables me to detect sounds and noises which the ordinary person does not hear.

36. I love great music and art, but I think 'cubist' songs and paintings are hideous.

37. Someday, man will harness the rise and fall of the tides, imprison the power of the sun, and release atomic power.

38. I am both pleased but astonished by the fact that mankind has not yet begun to use all the means and devices that are available for destruction. I hope that such weapons are never manufactured in quantity.

39. The United States, and other advanced nations, will someday be able to produce instruments of death so terrible the world will be in abject terror of itself and its ability to end

civilization. Such war-making weapons should be developed - butonly for purposes of discovery and experimentation

40. The dove is my emblem I want to save and advance human life, not destroy it.... I am proud of the fact that I never invented weapons to kill...

41. To me, the idea and expectation that the day is slowly and surely coming when we will be able to honestly say we are our brother's keeper and not his oppressor is very beautiful .

42. Until man duplicates a blade of grass, nature can laugh at his so-called scientific knowledge....

43. Its obvious that we don't know one millionth of one percent about anything.

44. I believe that the science of chemistry alone almost proves the existence of an intelligent creator.

45. We have merely scratched the surface of the store of knowledge which will come to us. I believe that we are now, a-tremble on the verge of vast discoveries - discoveries so wondrously important they will upset the present trend of human thought and start it along completely new lines .

46. Be courageous! Whatever setbacks America has encountered, it has always emerged as a stronger and more prosperous nation. Be brave as your fathers

before you. Have faith and go forward!

47. If parents pass enthusiasm along to their children, they will leave them an estate of incalculable value....

48. The memory of my mother will always be a blessing to me....

49. Life's most soothing things are a child's goodnight and sweet music....

50. Great music and art are earthly wonders, but I think 'cubist' songs and paintings are hideous.

51. Even though I am nearly deaf, I seem to be gifted with a kind of inner hearing which enables me to detect sounds and noises which the ordinary listener does not hear.